Mastering The Game

Winning From Within

Strategies For Lifelong Achievement

David Ambrose Jackson

While every effort has been made to ensure the accuracy and reliability of the information within this publication, the author assumes no responsibility or liability for any errors, omissions, or inconsistencies. The content provided is subject to change without notice and should not be interpreted as a definitive guide or source.

The information in this book is provided for educational and informational purposes only. The author has made every effort to ensure the accuracy and completeness of the content, drawing on personal research and knowledge in the fields of psychology and personal development, as well as the assistance of advanced technologies, including LLMs and research tools.

This material is not intended to diagnose, treat, or provide guidance on specific psychological or mental health conditions. The techniques, strategies, and practices discussed, particularly those related to subconscious-level training, are general insights for personal development. Individual results may vary, and no guarantees are made regarding the effectiveness of any methods described.

Readers are advised to use this information at their own discretion and assume full responsibility for any positive or negative outcomes—physical, mental, emotional, or otherwise—that may result from applying the strategies outlined in the book. If you have a pre-existing psychological condition or are experiencing significant emotional distress, it is strongly recommended to consult with a licensed mental health professional, therapist, or certified coach before implementing any of the suggestions.

This book is not a substitute for professional medical or psychological advice. Always seek the guidance of your physician or a qualified health provider with any concerns or questions about your mental or physical health.

The author disclaims any liability for loss, damage, or injury—whether direct or indirect—that may result from using or misusing the information provided. By reading this book, you acknowledge and agree to the terms of this disclaimer.

Contents

Introduction

The possibility I am inventing for myself, and my life is the unstoppable possibility of being a world-class, best-selling author whose words transform lives. I am the bold and powerful possibility of inspiring and igniting a global movement where people are empowered to elevate every area of their lives, creating breakthroughs in what matters most to them. D.A.J.

The idea for this book has been percolating for many years, both at a conscious and subconscious level. The original concept and ideas for the book were first consciously developed in 2012, but the foundational concept had existed for many years. The book is an exploration on a personal and professional level, testing concepts and ideas in the realm of personal development. It invites the reader to apply these concepts and ideas in their personal life, outlining several suggested areas for life development as we progress through the chapters. The book has been deeply reflected upon and designed to positively affect the reader through thoughtful consideration of each chapter at a subconscious level.

Indeed, suppose you are a student of personal and lifelong development. In that case, you may already have several areas of your life that you would like to enhance, increase, improve or expand upon. In the most recent idea generation of this book, two conceptual areas for exploration arose. Firstly, concept 1 is the *strategies of a chess master*, and secondly, concept 2 is *the power of the subconscious mind*. At this stage, I want to point out that this book is not about learning how to play the game of chess or the individual moves and rules of the game. Another point to outline is that this book will not explore the psychological nature of the subconscious mind, and the author does not claim to be an expert in either of these professions. The approach is based purely on research, observations, study, and personal and professional life experiences. A review of the author's bio will outline career skillsets and professional achievements for those interested and to appease the opponent.

You may approach this book from many perspectives. The recommended approach is to read the book from chapter to chapter, as the design is to educate and expand the subconscious mind with the core concepts before applying the various outlined stages. Essentially, it is a process of priming and engaging our subconscious mind to adapt to new and profound concepts that will bring about results.

This book's first edition results from a personal and professional goal. The second edition, however, will review the outcomes for both the author and those readers who wish to participate. The collective experiences gained from utilising the information presented in this book will be valuable to the development in the second edition.

Everything is possible if you believe it is possible. To test this theory, let's look at some very well-established quotes. Below we will see a common theme of beliefs, thoughts, limitations, dreams, and the courage to act:

"Believe you can, and you're halfway there."
Theodore Roosevelt (1858–1919).

"Whether you think you can or you think you can't, you're right."
Henry Ford (1863–1947).

"The only limit to our realisation of tomorrow, is our doubts of today."
Franklin D. Roosevelt (1882–1945).

"The future belongs to those who believe in the beauty of their dreams."
Eleanor Roosevelt (1884–1962).

"All our dreams can come true if we dare to pursue them."
Walt Disney (1901–1966).

As we will learn in this book, the seat for most of the programming of beliefs, thoughts, ideas, limits, and dreams is all stored in the subconscious mind. It is a good exercise to consider Henry Ford and Walt Disney as examples of what is possible to create in our lives. Look up some information about them on YouTube or do a Google search and see what comes up around their beliefs and achievements. Our world is enhanced by their creations when we think of the automobile industry, the world of cinema, and the various theme parks that open worlds of wonder, adventure, entertainment, and fun to all alike.

A word of note! The author does not intend to engage in any adverse political or otherwise held representation against any person represented here. The author does not want to challenge anyone's beliefs if they differ. The only purpose is to educate and empower the audience and readers who will benefit from the content presented herein.

Approaching training the subconscious mind like a game of chess is a creative and strategic analogy. Here's how the individual chess pieces could be represented, each symbolizing key elements of subconscious training:

1. King – The Conscious Mind

Role: The conscious mind governs decision-making, logic, and willpower. Just like the king in chess, it's crucial but limited in mobility.

Strategy: Protecting and guiding the king is vital, as its stability allows other pieces (mental faculties) to operate effectively. Training the subconscious mind starts with understanding and safeguarding the conscious mind's control over awareness and focus.

2. Queen – The Pineal Gland / Higher Creativity Center

Role: The most powerful piece, representing the pineal gland, the higher center of creativity, and the link between the conscious and subconscious minds. It symbolizes intuition, vision, and limitless potential.

Strategy: Use the queen to channel creativity, imagination, and intuition. Regular meditation, visualization, and affirmations involving the pineal gland help strengthen this connection and empower the subconscious mind.

3. Rooks – Habits and Repetition

Role: Rooks represent the power of structure, routines, and discipline, moving in straight lines like the routines that shape our daily behaviour.

Strategy: Create healthy, positive habits through repetition. The subconscious learns through consistency, so the rooks reinforce automatic behaviours that lead to desired outcomes.

4. Bishops – Emotions and Beliefs

Role: Bishops move diagonally, reflecting the subtle, indirect influence of emotions and deeply held beliefs on subconscious programming.

Strategy: Align emotions with your goals by fostering positive emotions and beliefs that resonate with your objectives. Emotional intelligence and self-awareness are key to influencing the subconscious.

5. Knights – Creativity and Problem-Solving

Role: Knights are agile, leaping over obstacles, representing creative thinking and problem-solving, crucial for training the subconscious mind to overcome challenges and see new possibilities.

Strategy: Use creativity to tackle limiting beliefs or mental barriers. The knight's unique movements remind you that breakthroughs often require unconventional thinking and mental flexibility.

6. Pawns – Affirmations and Positive Self-Talk

Role: Pawns are small but numerous, representing affirmations, positive self-talk, and small, consistent actions. Though they seem minor, they can advance and be promoted into powerful pieces over time.

Strategy: Use affirmations and self-suggestions daily to rewire the subconscious mind. Pawns may seem insignificant individually, but collectively, they create momentum and can transform into powerful outcomes with persistence.

7. Opponent's Pieces – Limiting Beliefs and Negative Thoughts

Role: The opposing pieces symbolize the obstacles in the form of limiting beliefs, negative thoughts, and external influences that challenge the process of subconscious training.

Strategy: Anticipate and counter these opposing forces with conscious awareness, emotional regulation, and strategic thinking. The better you defend against these negative patterns, the more empowered your subconscious becomes.

Overall Game Strategy:

Opening Moves: Start with awareness and mindfulness, setting intentions and identifying current mental habits. Build a strong foundation of positive self-talk (pawns) and emotional alignment (bishops).

Mid-Game: Gradually introduce complex strategies like visualization, meditation, and problem-solving (knights), while reinforcing positive habits (rooks). Continue aligning beliefs and emotions with desired outcomes.

End-Game: By this stage, your subconscious is more attuned to your conscious desires. Creativity and intuition (queen) play a central role as you transition deeper into manifesting goals.

By treating the subconscious like a chess game, you can approach it as a balanced, strategic effort where every move contributes to personal mastery. Enjoy the journey! David Ambrose Jackson.

Chapter 1

The Opponent

The intention of Chapter 1, The Opponent, is to stimulate a shift in your perspective by highlighting that the primary obstacle to achieving success is not factors but rather your own subconscious minds influence. This chapter encourages you to address your thoughts and emotional reactions that may be constraining your growth potential. By engaging in self-reflection and practicing mindfulness techniques outlined in this section you can uncover the core beliefs that dictate your behaviours and choices. The process offers you a chance to reframe your mindset and behaviours for a fulfilling life experience. The objective is to inspire you to develop approaches to living, that promote liberty and choice while achieving exceptional outcomes in every aspect of your life.

Have you ever woken up each morning with a feeling that you're not reaching your true potential in life? Maybe you feel stuck in your career? Are facing challenges in relationships? Do you often hear a persistent inner voice telling you that you're not capable enough? Consider this, what if the biggest barrier to your success is not the external obstacles you face but a hidden adversary, within yourself? What if your own subconscious mind is the opponent holding you back?

Before facing this challenge head on, it requires you to focus on understanding your behaviour patterns in a meaningful way from within yourself. Observe the times when you find yourself reacting emotionally in ways repeatedly – be it feeling nervous before public speaking or getting annoyed in specific social situations. Recognising these recurring reactions provides an initial insight into the workings of your subconscious mind. Whenever you respond in a manner to a situation it is like a signpost – a message, from your subconscious mind that gives you an opportunity to acknowledge and harness that awareness as your strength.

Regularly jotting down your feelings and reflections can be a way to recognise these patterns effectively. Take a moment each day to document your experiences and think about the emotions you experienced in different situations. You will eventually observe themes. Similar feelings connected to certain triggers. This exercise is not about being critical of yourself but, about being mindful and compassionate. Begin by acknowledging your thoughts without attempting to modify them and always remember to treat yourself kindly along the way.

Have you ever thought about what occurs before you start feeling anxious or frustrated? What are the things that set off these emotions for you? It could be a comment someone made or an approaching deadline or even how a particular person behaves around you that triggers these feelings in you initially. It is essential to recognise and comprehend the situations that lead to these emotional responses as this marks the beginning of self-awareness – the core of altering your subconscious mind effectively. The key is to keep practicing this awareness because with time and repetition it becomes clearer that these patterns of emotions are not fixtures but rather familiar occurrences in your life. Once you've identified them for what they are and acknowledge their presence in your life, consistently, only then can you begin the process of making changes, for the better.

The unconscious mind holds power in shaping your thoughts and actions which in turn influences the course of your life journey, silently in the background like a puppet master, pulling strings without you even realising it. Over time your mind retains every bit of information such as, negative remarks, cultural influences, social norms and childhood memories, all stored within your subconscious realm. This hidden reservoir is often the origin of self-doubt, fear of failure and a fixed mindset that hinders growth.

Imagine taking a moment to ponder a dream or goal you've always had but never pursued before visualising it clearly in your mind's eye. What does it look like and how does owning it make you feel inside? Now pay attention to the thoughts and feelings that arise. Are they positive at first or do doubts and negativity creep in quickly? Do you hear voices questioning your capabilities with remarks, like *"Who do you think you are to attempt this?". "You're not capable of achieving that?".*

Reflecting on occurrences triggers thoughts about the feasibility of your ambitions right away for you too? Have you felt a rush of discomfort and self-doubt wash over you? This exercise offers a glimpse, into how your subconscious mind operates. Acting as a sieve that sifts through your concerns, rooted beliefs and past encounters to influence each choice you make. When pessimism creeps in your subconscious erects barriers, often drawing from norms, past errors and opinions accumulated over the years.

You need to understand this. Your subconscious mind is not against you, however, it could hinder you if left unchecked. It functions automatically based on outdated rules and unexamined beliefs. But here's the good news. You have the power to change those patterns. You can start dismantling the barriers created by your programming simply by being aware. Begin questioning those responses that pop up unconsciously. Of accepting them blindly ask yourself *"Is this belief helping me move forward or holding me back?"* Taking on this challenge marks the beginning of your journey, towards transformation.

Your inner self protects your capabilities within you. To unlock your potential and achieve greatness in life, one must first acknowledge and understand this hidden adversary. The initial move, towards change begins with being mindful and conscious of your surroundings and actions.

Your subconscious plays a role in your everyday life instead of just being a passive bystander. It often influences your behaviours and emotions without you even realising it consciously. This process usually starts at an age when your mind is highly receptive to the messages from those around you – parents, teachers and the society at large. If you grew up hearing that you were not intelligent or not as good as others those beliefs likely became deeply rooted in your thoughts. Over time these concepts solidify into a mindset that makes you fearful of failure and hesitant to embrace change or face rejection.

Contrary to a growth mindset that believes in the potential for skill development and improvement over time a fixed mindset asserts that your abilities are set in stone. It aims to convince you that your shortcomings are a part of you. If you encounter failure you may hesitate to tackle challenges out of fear of impacting how you see yourself. This mindset does not simply emerge out of nowhere. Often traces back to early experiences where achievements, responses and acceptance were viewed as contingent upon certain conditions.

Growing up in a society with social and cultural influences can reinforce these patterns of behaviour even more significantly. At times when your upbringing places an emphasis on fitting in with the crowd having thoughts that seem unconventional or risky may trigger warning signals from your subconscious mind. In communities that prioritise performance and ideal standards you might find yourself haunted by worries of judgment or fixated on unattainable levels of perfection. These concerns could lead you to procrastinate tasks as a way to protect yourself emotionally.

As you start to become more aware of your feelings and emotions in situations and contexts it is important to dig deeper into understanding them better. Once you've identified the situations that evoke emotional reactions within, you ask yourself what kind of emotions they are. Do you find yourself feeling angry or anxious or sad in scenarios? For instance, certain individuals might consistently make you feel inadequate or certain places could always make you feel uneasy. Make a note of these emotions when they arise as paying attention to these subtle nuances can help you uncover what lies beneath the surface.

In addition to identifying situations, around you it is important to be aware of your thoughts. Those immediate negative thoughts that arise involuntarily in your mind. When faced with a situation these thoughts can appear automatically such *as "I am not capable enough"* or *"I tend to make mistakes always"*. These automatic thoughts reflect beliefs you hold about yourself which influence your actions. For example, if you have a belief that you are bound to fail it will influence every decision and action you make.

Let's dive deeper and sketch the trends you've begun to observe. When a situation like *"A"* arises for me (to your *"B"*) I often experience *"C"* feelings and tend to respond by doing *"D"*. For instance, when you're dealing with a time constraint (A) you might sense stress (C) and delay tasks (D). These sequences of thoughts and emotions followed by actions can be quite intriguing. Comprehending how they work grants you authority, over your conduct. You might come across beliefs such, as *"Feeling unworthy"* or *"Believing I won't achieve success"*, which could influence these behaviours.

Imagining these situations could give you some perspective! Take a time each day to picture the moments that tend to set off your automatic reactions without you even realising it. You should ask yourself how you feel during those times and what your usual reaction is like. By immersing yourself in this exercise and envision a new and more empowering way of responding, you have the opportunity to alter how things unfold.

Let's delve deeper into this topic and think about those times when you tend to doubt yourself with thoughts, like *"Am I not disciplined"*. *"Why do I always seem to mess things up?"*. Take a moment to reflect on the origins of these beliefs. When did you first start feeling this way about yourself and what might have contributed to it?

What emotions did that evoke for you. Did it trigger any memories you hadn't considered before? These ingrained beliefs are often tied to specific events or recurring situations that once appeared to confirm our deepest insecurities. You can start recognising these notions for what they are by tracing their origins. Outdated assumptions formed from limited knowledge rather than undeniable truths, about your current self.

Now that you're aware of where it came from let's talk about the belief itself. Just because something felt real to you in the past does not mean it has to feel that way now or in the future. Share an experience from your life that challenges this idea. For example, if you struggle with staying focused and disciplined at times think back to moments when you tackled a task or completed a project with grit and determination. Remember that growth and change are possible regardless of what your inner fears may suggest. It is not about being perfect. Your beliefs can change. They're not fixed forever in place. By understanding where they come from you can transform these patterns. Your past doesn't have to dictate your future.

We've explored how your subconscious mind influences your perception of the world without you realising it consciously. Your subconscious has been moulding your self-esteem and confidence based on signals received since childhood and influenced by your background. These seated beliefs can manifest as procrastination tendencies or a fear of failure among other self-sabotaging behaviours. The key takeaway here is that the crucial first step to overcoming these patterns, is being aware of them. Transforming your life is within reach, when you delve into the depths of your mind and embrace a new way of thinking.

Let's wrap things up with a task that brings everything into perspective! Pick one goal or change you want to work towards in your life. Jot it down first. Note down any negative or doubtful thoughts that pop into your mind when you think about achieving this goal. Then comes the interesting part—write down a counter belief for each negative thought! These should reflect your potential, for growth and success. For example, If one of your thoughts is *"Maybe I'm not skilled enough"* the counter belief could be *"There's always room for me to improve and learn new things every day."*

Give yourself a moment to reflect on this assignment. What stood out to you? Had a significant impact? How did it feel when you compared your thoughts to positive ones? Remember that this is more than a task—it's about reshaping your subconscious mind. By choosing new and empowering beliefs you have the power to transform your mindset from one of restrictions, to one filled with opportunities.

As you progress in your journey of retraining your mind remember that it is an ongoing process and not just a onetime event. Be patient with yourself. When old beliefs resurface recognise them as remnants of the past instead of indicators of your future. Replace them with new positive thoughts that resonate with the person you aspire to be. Surround yourself with supportive individuals, places and literature that reinforce your newfound mindset. Most importantly take small steps, towards your goals without hesitation. The effective way to overcome fear and persuade your inner mind that you are capable of making changes is to take action.

After exploring these patterns and reflecting on your responses in depth. It is a good idea to begin keeping a thorough record of your thoughts and feelings over an extended period of time. Maybe for a week or even a month! Over time you will observe recurring patterns not in what sets you off, but also in how your reactions develop over time.

When you're feeling a certain way, *"Why am I feeling like this?"* and *"What does this remind me of?"*, are some questions to ponder over. There's depth to these questions as they lead you to delve into the underlying reasons behind your reactions. Often these emotions are tied to childhood memories or impactful moments that have influenced your mindset. Start questioning those negative thoughts. For instance, when a discouraging thought such, as *"I'm"* arises challenge it by asking yourself, *"Is this really accurate?", "What proof do I possess to back up or challenge this?"* By interrogating these ideas in your mind's eye' you begin to ease the hold they exert on your actions.

Identify the root fears that drive your responses. Are they rooted in fear of rejection or failure or, in feelings of inadequacy? Acknowledgment of deep-seated fears empowers you to confront them directly. The better you comprehend the origins of thoughts and their triggers the more effectively you can begin to question and combat them proactively.

Think about more than your usual habits – picture yourself in a challenging scenario and see yourself responding in a new way, calmly and confidently with a clear mind. This practice of preparing yourself could help reframe how you face future obstacles.

Your inner thoughts have silently influenced your opinions and actions over time without you realising it as they lurked in the background like a secret rival all along. Now you've come face to face with this opponent and what's more significant is that you have the power to transform it. By being aware of your programming and actively challenging it while choosing new beliefs intentionally will enable you to break free from the constraints of your past. Your past does not dictate your future. Right at this moment, is when you can alter the path of your fate.

Summary & Practice

To deeply connect with your thoughts and begin transforming deeply ingrained beliefs and behaviours. Here are the essential actions you can follow.

- Notice familiar emotional trends.
- Take note of moments when you find yourself reacting emotionally like feeling anxious or frustrated.
- Notice the ways in which these emotions show up in parts of your life.
- Make it a habit to write down your thoughts and feelings regularly.
- Pay attention to what triggers your responses and keep an eye out for patterns.
- Engage in mindfulness exercises.
- Take a moment every day to just sit with your thoughts.
- Pay attention to what comes up without any prejudice to comprehend your reflex reactions.
- Grasp Emotional Trends.
- Recognise how you react in situations like when "Event A" happens. Make sure to outline these patterns either in your mind or, on paper to gain an understanding of them.

- Identifying Negative Thoughts.
- Pay attention to any thoughts that come up in your mind when you wake up in the morning.
- Keep in mind that these usually mirror beliefs that impact your decisions.
- Question your assumptions.
- Whenever a negative thought crosses your mind take a moment to question its validity by asking yourself *"Is this thought accurate?"*
- Think about the proof that either backs up or goes against this idea to transform it into something optimistic.
- Imagine various reactions.
- Each day brings moments that stir up reactions and feelings from the past.
- Imagine yourself replying with calmness and assurance instead.
- Recognise the fears that influence how people react.
- Identify the fears, such, as the fear of failure or rejection that drive our subconscious responses.
- Reveal these anxieties to understand and manage your habits better.
- Ponder.
- Remember to jot down your thoughts and emotions as they evolve through time.
- Look through the data to find patterns or cues that can provide valuable information insights.
- Practice patience.
- Show empathy.

It's important to remember that changing habits doesn't happen overnight. Setbacks are all part of the process. Be kind, to yourself as you strive for transformation. Remember to track your thoughts and feelings over time noting any recurring patterns or triggers through reviews of your records. This ongoing reflection can provide valuable insights into your innermost thoughts and emotions, over the long run.

Remember to be patient and show compassion to yourself as you work on reshaping your habits over time. Progress takes time and setbacks are a natural part of the journey, towards change.

Chapter 2

Contemplation

The intention of Chapter 2, Contemplation, is to shift your focus for personal growth rather than relying on external sources for change. This chapter encourages self-exploration of your world, encompassed by thoughts and emotions to pave the way for transformative experiences. By engaging in activities such as, journal writing and mindfulness practices while fostering self-dialogue techniques, you will unlock new perspectives that empower you to make intentional choices in your journey of self-discovery. The goal is to move from reacting automatically to responding with purposeful intention so that you can harmonise your internal thoughts with the results you seek.

Have you ever thought about delving within yourself as the key to unlocking your true capabilities instead of acquiring new skills and knowledge externally? Imagine focusing to explore the landscape of your thoughts and emotions rather than searching for answers outside. Personal growth and transformation begin with self-awareness—it is like switching on the light in a room. You start to notice the obstacles and opportunities that have always been present but overlooked.

Embark on your path to self-discovery by observing the recurring patterns in your thoughts and actions. Whether it's the nervousness, before speaking publicly or the discomfort felt in bustling environments. These reactions hold significance beyond mere chance. They stem from your subconscious workings influenced by deep rooted beliefs and past events. Take note of these tendencies as acknowledging them marks the stride towards comprehending how your subconscious impacts your everyday existence.

To enhance your self-awareness on a level and gain insights into your inner world better, you can incorporate journaling into your routine. It can truly help you understand yourself more comprehensively, by jotting down your thoughts and feelings regularly, as it allows you to capture the nuances of your inner experiences. This practice can assist you in recognising patterns between different events and how you react emotionally to them. Over time you might begin to recognise specific triggers such as a challenging day at work that repeatedly evoke feelings of insecurity or anxiety. By maintaining a journal you create a roadmap, towards unravelling the hidden layers of your subconscious mind.

Moreover, someone can find it helpful to practice mindfulness in this situation. Take a few moments every day to observe your thoughts without any bias or criticism. Whether you choose to concentrate on your breathing or how your body feels this routine helps create some space between your thoughts and your responses. When faced with an irritated thought take note of it without instantly reacting. This brief moment of reflection can change your outlook enabling you to handle life's difficulties with consideration. Here, in this realm of existence you are no longer an observer of your feelings – you start to influence your subconscious mind actively.

Engaged by rooted beliefs and routine thinking patterns cruising on autopilot mode comes naturally in our everyday routines. Often unaware of the urges that influence our actions we tend to react instinctively rather than reflect. Just picture this. What if you could pause, step back and comprehend the underlying reasons behind your thoughts and behaviours? This section will guide you through practices of self-awareness and reflection allowing you to connect with your mind in ways that empower and positively impact you. Let's explore techniques such as encouraging self-talk, being present in the moment, writing in a journal and creating images. Practices that can illuminate your true self and guide you toward personal growth.

Let's start off with an exercise, close your eyes and take a few deep breaths in and out slowly. Think back, to a time recently when you felt irritated or overwhelmed. As you think about that moment again now... What thoughts come to mind? Are there any self-frustrated words running through your head? Now picture if a friend was going through the situation. How would you comfort or encourage them? Try replacing your self-thoughts with positive and uplifting phrases during your reflection time.

Reflect on the outcomes of that experience and consider your reactions. Did you lean towards self-criticism or negativity at first glance? How did it feel to replace those thoughts with words of encouragement? This simple shift exemplifies the importance of self-awareness and positive self-talk. Often our automatic response is to be harder on ourselves than we would be on others. Recognising this tendency is the step towards challenging and changing it.

Positive self-talk is a tool for transforming your inner dialogue and consequently shaping your reality beyond just feeling good about it all. The words you speak to yourself matter as they impact your mindset and actions along with your overall sense of self-worth, significantly. Begin incorporating sessions of positive self-talk into your routine and when you notice negative self-talk creeping in take a moment to pause and reframe the narrative. Replace thoughts like *" I can't do this "* with encouraging ones such as *" I am, in the process of learning; making mistakes is a natural part of growth."* Consistent practice will help ingrain these affirmations as your mental narrative and building up your mindset and inner strength.

The initial phase, in improvement involves developing self-awareness, where shifting your mindset from limitation to possibility begins with recognising your internal dialogue and maintaining a positive self-narrative consistently. This section aims to equip you with tools to enhance your self-awareness and leverage introspection for enduring change.

Increasing self-awareness involves observing your thoughts and emotions and exploring the ingrained patterns of your mind. The practice of mindfulness meditation is a tool that can help you achieve this heightened level of awareness. By being fully present in the moment without passing judgment mindfulness allows you to view your thoughts and feelings as temporary and separate from yourself. This perspective enables you to detach yourself from them.

Why is this important to consider? Having awareness aids in giving yourself room, for thought before reacting. You transition from reacting to responding purposefully. This shift can impact aspects of your life such as how you handle stress and approach achieving goals.

On the side, meditation serves as a method to train the mind to focus, relax, and establish a deeper connection with your inner being over time. Engaging in regular meditation can reduce stress, increase self-understanding, and aid in discovering greater balance and peace within oneself. It is like a workout that boosts your ability to observe your thoughts without letting them dominate you.

Give this a shot. Take a moment for some mindfulness meditation here with me! Start by closing your eyes and finding a spot to sit comfortably at ease while taking a deep breath in and out slowly and smoothly. Focus on the sensation of your breath as it moves in and out of your body—notice how your chest gently rises and falls with each inhale and exhale as you feel the air entering and exiting through your nose. If your mind starts to wander off track during this practice session gently guide it back to the rhythm of your breathing without any judgment—just observe passing thoughts like clouds drifting across the sky. Let these thoughts flow in and out naturally like waves while consistently redirecting your attention back, to the rhythm of your breath.

How did you feel during that time to yourself? Did you find moments of calmness? Practicing mindfulness doesn't require clearing your mind or achieving total silence. It's gently guiding your thoughts back, to the present moment once you notice them drifting away. Consistent mindfulness practice enables you to observe your thoughts than letting them control you.

Engaging in mindfulness and meditation practices can enhance one's inner strength over time by starting with just a few minutes each day and gradually increasing the duration as you become more comfortable with it. The goal is not perfection but personal growth. Try to bring mindfulness to daily activities like eating meals or doing household chores. The more you incorporate these practices into your routine and develop a sense of self-awareness through them, the better equipped you'll be to recognise and change any unproductive behaviours that arise.

Two key tools for achieving self-awareness are mindfulness and meditation. They allow you to create space for intentional than automatic responses and enhance your connection, with your inner self. Mastering these practices helps you become an empathetic observer of your thoughts and feelings making way for meaningful transformation.

As you work on developing self-awareness techniques into your routine it's important to dig deeper into your emotions. Begin by recognising the feelings associated with circumstances. Do locations or encounters regularly elicit emotions such as anxiety, anger or sadness? These emotional reactions serve as clues to revealing beliefs buried in your subconscious. For instance, a specific social environment could trigger feelings of insecurity due to experiences where you felt criticised or left out.

When you find yourself in these situations or moments of uncertainty or challenge – take note of the thoughts that pop up in your mind such as *"Am I capable enough?"* or *"This won't work out."* These rapid thoughts usually hold beliefs regarding yourself and the world around you. Beliefs that influence your actions subtly without you realising it fully yet when you become aware of these instant reactions coming from within you. It provides a window into the inner narratives that your subconscious runs on.

Trying to sort out these ideas? Consider drawing a diagram of your trends to see how your thoughts and feelings influence each other visually. For example, if getting criticism makes you feel inadequate and then causes you to shy away, from taking on challenges. You might be stuck in a repetitive loop. By sketching out these trends visually helps you understand how your subconscious influences your responses and gives you the chance to change these patterns.

Delving further into the matter involves pondering the convictions that influence your behaviours significantly. When you find yourself grappling with feelings of inadequacy or apprehension of failure frequently it could signify a rooted belief regarding self-value. Grasping these beliefs can lead to changes as it allows you to realise that they may not be absolute truths but rather narratives stemming from past encounters.

As you delve further into your journey of self-discovery it's essential to not acknowledge the patterns but also grasp the emotions and automatic thoughts that stem from them. Keeping a journal serves as a tool for enhancing self-awareness. One reflective practice that allows you to systematically delve into your thoughts and emotions is writing. Engaging in the act of putting thoughts on paper is akin to having a conversation with oneself. It is more than documenting your day. Writing aids in structuring your thoughts and helps in analysing experiences as well as identifying patterns in behaviour.

Journaling is a practice because it engages various parts of your brain allowing you to delve into deeper thoughts and emotions effectively. It also aids in slowing down your thought process enabling you to see things from new perspectives and navigate through challenging feelings more easily. Having a journal helps in documenting your inner journey and assists in monitoring your progress over time.

Start by opening a document on your computer or take out a notebook to write in it freely for five minutes without worrying about spelling or punctuation on a topic that interests you, or something you've been pondering about lately. After five minutes. Go through what you've written reflecting on what stands out to you the most. Notice any patterns, recurring themes or insights that you may have discovered while writing.

Putting your thoughts on paper can lead to revelations and insights that may have escaped your conscious awareness. It can bring to light aspirations fears and recurring narratives that shape how you see the world. Developing self-awareness hinges largely on this introspective exercise as it allows you to gain a deeper understanding of your inner landscape

Journal writing doesn't have to be complicated or time consuming. It can be a practice that brings about meaningful changes in your self-awareness with just a few minutes each day.

Start by asking yourself questions *like "How am I feeling today and why?"* or *"What small step can I take today to get closer to my goals?"* Regular journal entries can assist you in monitoring your progress staying connected to your aspirations and providing a space for exploring your thoughts and emotions.

Journal writing is a tool, for self-reflection and growth providing a space to explore your thoughts and experiences gain clarity and reshape the narratives that shape your life according to your true self.

One highly successful approach to enhancing self-awareness and aligning your subconscious thoughts with your conscious goals is through visualisation techniques. Visualising the outcomes you desire creates mental images of them. This vivid imagery helps engage your subconscious in a manner that renders these goals more plausible and achievable. Practicing this exercise can boost your self-assurance motivate you and help you stay focused, on your goals.

Why is vision so impactful? The mind often struggles to distinguish between imagined occurrences using familiar neural pathways for both scenarios – whether you're envisioning a positive result or experiencing it firsthand. This does not boost your self-assurance, in achieving your goals it also enhances your mental acuity in recognising opportunities and aligns your actions accordingly.

Imagine yourself with your eyes closed envision a future self who has achieved a goal to you as vividly as possible, imagining yourself in the clothes you are currently wearing, and your surroundings take note of the sights sounds and even the scents surrounding you. Make this mental image detailed and vibrant spend some time embracing this visualisation before gently opening your eyes.

How did you feel about that visualisation task I shared earlier with you. Did it stir up any emotions or insights for you? Visualising can be a motivator as it allows you to connect emotionally with your goals making them feel more attainable and real rather than just abstract thoughts. By visualising your desired outcomes, you keep your subconscious focused, on your aspirations instead of dwelling on fears or uncertainties.

Adding visualisation to your routine can enhance productivity and overall wellbeing significantly. Dedicate a few moments each morning or evening visualising the achievement of your goals as if they are already happening. Combine this practice with affirmations such, as *" I am confident and capable "* or *" I am effortlessly reaching my goals."* The clearer and vividly you can picture your success in your mind's eye, the more effectively your subconscious will work towards manifesting it into reality.

A key connection between where you want to go in life and where you're now lies in visualisation practice. Consistently engaging in this activity can align your thoughts with your external desires resulting in making your dreams feel more attainable and within reach. Visualisation techniques along with affirmations, and encouraging self-talk form a powerful trio that can guide you on the journey to self-discovery and growth.

When you reach a level of self-awareness and start questioning and changing these underlying patterns consciously is when you truly grow as a person. To begin this process keeping a journal of your thoughts and feelings for an extended period. Be it daily or weekly, is crucial. By observing these patterns over time you'll notice recurring themes in your emotions and actions that will offer you insights, into the hidden influences affecting your choices.

Ask yourself profound questions about the feelings you're having like *"What's causing me to feel this?"* and *"Does this emotion bring up any memories for me?"* Emotions are commonly linked to past events such as experiences from childhood or important moments in your life. When you dig deeper into the origins of your emotions you can understand how past events are still influencing your actions and thoughts today.

Questioning thoughts is essential in this process too. You shouldn't just take them at face value as they arise in your mind, but rather examine their validity by asking yourself if they are truly accurate or what evidence you have for or against them instead. By challenging these thoughts and replacing them with more positive alternatives you can change the way you see yourself and reduce their impact on your actions.

Dig further to uncover the deep-seated fears that influence your subconscious behaviours—it could be the dread of rejection or failure or feeling inadequate in some way. Recognising and acknowledging these fears enables you to address them head on and diminish their influence, on how you act and decide.

Put your visualisation skills to use in situations as well! Picturing your current reactions in your mind's eye, try envision yourself reacting differently in future scenarios instead. Imagine yourself managing a meeting or social encounter, with composure and assurance. This practice doesn't just reconfigure your brain, it also equips you for actual situations where you could put these fresh responses into action.

When you question your beliefs and confront your inner fears while imagining different reactions to situations you gain power over the deep-seated patterns in your mind that influence you subconsciously. Self-awareness and reflection form the core of growth. In this chapter we have explored techniques like positive self-talk, mindfulness, meditation, keeping a journal, and visualisation, that could enable you to unlock your abilities and establish a connection with your subconscious mind. These methods assist in addressing thoughts and allowing your ideas and emotions to flow without criticism while aligning your actions, with your true goals.

Let's make a plan for ourselves as we wrap up this chapter together! As you reflect on what we've covered so far in this chapter about developing positive habits, like self-affirmation or mindfulness practice, writing or visualisation that resonated with you the most, and share how you plan to integrate it into your daily routine moving forward. For example, if you choose to journal, commit to spending five minutes every morning jotting down your thoughts. If mindfulness is your pick, allocate specific time each day for meditation or conscious breathing exercises.

Reflect on your commitment. What led you to choose this routine for yourself. How will incorporating it into your life benefit you in achieving your goals? Consider how this routine can enhance your self-awareness and help you approach your targets. Outline any obstacles you anticipate and strategies for overcoming them. If finding time proves challenging, could setting a reminder or integrating the routine with an existing habit such as enjoying morning coffee be helpful?

Always remember that maintaining consistency is crucial when you begin implementing these concepts into your routine or practice. Your journey towards improvement may encounter challenges and doubts in the early stages. In such times of struggle or hesitation treat yourself with kindness and acknowledge that progress is a continuous process rather than a final goal. If there are days where you falter or feel disheartened, gently steer yourself back on track without being too hard on yourself. Celebrate the smallest achievements and appreciate your growth no matter how insignificant it may seem at first glance.

Exploring self-awareness is like embarking on a journey of growth than reaching a destination in life's path. By practicing habits such as encouraging self-talk and mindfulness and engaging in writing and visualisation exercises regularly, these practices can empower you to navigate through life with strength and clarity while staying true to your purpose. Remember that the profound journey you'll ever take is the one within yourself. Understanding your nature enables you to uncover your potential for growth and development and live a life that aligns with your true capabilities. One mindful step, at a time will lead you forward gracefully on this path.

Summary & Practice

Getting to know yourself on a level starting from, within.

- Understand recurring trends in ideas and behaviours.
- Make sure you keep a journal to jot down and reflect on your experiences.
- Practice mindfulness, by observing your thoughts without passing any judgment on them.
- Think about the factors that trigger reactions.
- Ask simple questions to understand the responses better.
- Improve comprehension.
- Automatically detect cues and recognise recurring thoughts.
- Develop depictions of patterns to showcase how thoughts and emotions influence actions.
- Discover the underlying principles that shape behavioural inclinations.
- Visualise scenarios using pictures.
- Use visualisation to imagine and practice your reactions.
- Keep an eye on trends, over a period to get a grasp of consistent behaviour patterns.
- Strengthen your understanding.
- Explore the fundamental roots of your feelings.
- Challenge pessimism, by examining whether those thoughts hold merit or not.
- Explore the fears that lurk beneath reflecting on how past events have influenced your beliefs and behaviour.

By incorporating these habits into your routine, you can enhance your understanding of yourself and embark on the journey of harmonising your unconscious thoughts with your conscious aspirations. Keep in mind that self-awareness is not a stop but an ongoing adventure of self-discovery and development.

Chapter 3

Resources

The intention of Chapter 3 - Resources, is to empower you to make long lasting changes by understanding that your subconscious patterns play a crucial role in shaping your life, beyond just external actions and strategies alone. In this chapter you are encouraged to delve into methods, like Cognitive Behavioural Therapy (CBT) Neuro Linguistic Programming (NLP) and Emotional Freedom Techniques (EFT) as ways to adjust deeply rooted behaviours. By using these techniques effectively among others, you can overcome viewpoints and reflexive responses by making deliberate decisions that support your objectives. The main goal is to empower yourself to purposefully plan your life instead of being controlled by unconscious habits.

This chapter suggests utilising the professional support of accredited and licensed practitioners in the fields of counselling, psychotherapy, and coaching at various levels and disciplines. It is not essential at the foundational level or indeed the advanced levels depending upon the level of introspective work you may have done or indeed are presently engaged in. Sometimes to get a deeper perspective on our selves we can benefit from the assistance of someone who will act as a sounding board or a supportive friend. The main thing is to surround your self with people who will support your journey. If you are triggered by something or have experienced deep traumatic experiences in your life, it is ok, you are not alone, countless people unfortunately have been in your shoes or are presently there. Life ebbs and flows and we don't have to look to far to see people overcoming very difficult circumstances daily. That is what separates us from artificial life, our abilities to overcome challenges, whether personal or business related or both. The key point here is to use help when you identify that you need it. Let's review some possible resources open to you, this is not and exhaustive list but just some related fields that will be beneficial in supporting our theme.

Imagine if delving into the ingrained patterns of your subconscious could unlock the door to a life makeover of simply striving for fresh goals or embracing new tactics for change. Picture yourself conquering hurdles and experiencing substantial personal development through innovative approaches to thoughts and actions. Therapy and coaching serve as paths toward this kind of transformation, by equipping you with methods and skills that catalyse profound shifts at a core level.

Before delving into the methods for making changes in your life habits and behaviours it's crucial to initially nurture self-awareness. This marks the starting point of the process at hand. Take note of how your current actions and thought processes may be running on autopilot mode, due to ingrained subconscious beliefs. By observing recurring thoughts and feelings along with your responses, to situations you can begin to discern underlying patterns that influence your actions. For example, if you catch yourself putting things off or engaging in self-talk take a moment to reflect on when these tendencies tend to surface and what triggers them.

Keeping a journal of your thoughts and emotions routinely can be a method to recognise these patterns in your life. When you jot down your experiences you start to notice how particular feelings or convictions connect to occurrences or circumstances. For instance, maybe your tendency to delay tasks emerges whenever you confront an assignment stemming from an underlying fear of failing. As you record your ideas pay attention to the cues that spark these reactions. This can offer you a glimpse into your thoughts.

One important technique for improving self-awareness is practice. Take a few moments every day to pay attention to your thoughts without passing judgment on them. Become aware of your reactions right away to negative thoughts or habits that surface in your mind try just observing them calmly. By doing this you can create a distance between your thoughts and your responses, giving you the power to act with more purpose.

In this section we will explore a variety of methods and strategies designed to assist you in reshaping your thoughts and beliefs effectively. Behaviour Modification Approaches, Choice Theory Reality Therapy, Cognitive Behavioural Strategies (CBT) Neuro Linguistic Programming (NLP) Emotional Freedom Techniques (EFT), Tapping and Hypnosis. Each of these methods offers unique approaches to address and modify hidden patterns that may hinder your personal growth and development. Harnessing these methods can support you in creating enduring transformations and aligning your behaviours with your desired outcomes.

When delving into these techniques for self-improvement and growth it's important to go deeper than just scratching the surface and delve into understanding the emotional cues and ingrained thought patterns that shape your actions accordingly. For example, Choice Theory by Dr. William Glasser underlines the significance of pinpointing the desires fuelling your actions – be it, for affection, authority or independence. When applying Choice Theory ponder over this question; *What desire am I aiming to fulfil through this action?* For instance, if you're indulging excessively in food or spending much time on social media it could be a way to seek comfort or assert control.

When you understand the reasons behind your actions and behaviours you can start outlining your routines. Imagine how your thoughts, feelings and behaviours link together in a loop. For instance, if you delay a task **(action)** you could experience worry **(emotion)** due to your concerns, about not succeeding **(thought)**. This practice lets you recognise the underlying beliefs influencing your behaviours and gives you a view of what requires modification.

In the realm of Cognitive Behavioural Therapy (CBT) this mapping process can extend deeper into understanding one's thoughts and behaviours on a personal level. There is a strong focus on the interconnection between thoughts, moods and actions in CBT. It aims to help you pinpoint and confront harmful thought patterns that may exist within you. Imagine believing *"I am not worthy"* (a thought) this in turn could stir up feelings of inadequacy, in you (emotion) eventually leading to avoidance of tasks that challenge you (action). As you become aware of this recurring pattern you can take steps to disrupt it by replacing beliefs with more rational ones.

When you organise these observations systematically you develop a grasp of the motivations shaping your actions. This awareness empowers you to make decisions that are informed and impactful.

To enhance our comprehension of behaviour modification techniques is to start with an exercise. Think about a habit or behaviour you'd like to change—whether its negative self-talk or procrastination or making healthier choices in life. Close your eyes. Imagine how you could alter this habit by replacing it with a more positive behaviour instead. Envision yourself embracing this beneficial habit, for example, if you're envisioning overcoming procrastination picture yourself actively engaged in work and feeling accomplished. Take note of the emotions and sensations that arise as you consider this empowering transformation.

Remember when you visualised it in your mind's eye and reflected on it later. What did you notice about the feelings and thoughts that arose when you thought about actions. How did this compare to your usual interactions with this routine. Frequently observing the desired transformation can make you recognise how distinct it is from your current situation It highlights the contrast, between where you want to be and where you currently are which can help you pinpoint the challenges and incentives involved.

The initial step to bring about change involves recognising the disparity, between your actions and desired results. Begin by setting achievable goals that will steer you towards your intended behaviour to bridge this gap. For instance, in overcoming procrastination break down tasks into segments and set short deadlines. Acknowledge each achievement to build momentum and encourage the modified behaviour. Remember that staying consistent is key and transformation happens over time.

Coaching and counselling provides a framework, for shifting patterns and behaviours enabling individuals to envision desired changes and understand the process of behavioural change ultimately setting the stage for implementing effective strategies that lead to lasting transformation.

Let's explore some techniques that can assist in making changes to behaviour patterns – including Choice Theory and Reality Therapy by Dr. William Glasser. According to Choice Theory our desires for love, power, freedom and enjoyment serve, as driving factors. This viewpoint suggests that the actions we take are choices made to fulfil these needs. Building upon Choice Theory Reality Therapy focuses on guiding individuals towards making choices to fulfil their needs and improve their overall wellbeing.

Why is this important? Choice Theory and Reality Therapy emphasise the significance of choice and accountability encouraging individuals to take ownership of their actions and acknowledge their ability to change their behaviour patterns. By recognising the underlying needs that influence your actions you are empowered to make decisions that align with your beliefs and goals, in a mindful manner.

Think about a habit you'd like to change up a bit. What was the motivation behind it in the first place? If you find yourself overdoing something like snacking much or spending too much screen time scrolling through social media feeds. That could indicate a need for reassurance or relaxation perhaps. Take a moment to note down this behaviour along with the reason driving it. Next up. Brainstorm some actions that could better fulfil this underlying need or desire. For instance, if what you're really craving is some comfort and ease. Consider unwinding in a soothing bath or catching up with a pal instead.

Consider reflecting on the requirements you identified and the alternative courses of action you proposed previously. Do any insights or unexpected discoveries come to light when pondering this further? Recognising the core needs driving your behaviour allows you to address the root cause than just addressing surface level issues. This awareness also empowers you to make informed decisions on how to fulfil your desires without resorting to harmful or unproductive behaviours.

Use Choice Theory and Reality Therapy to focus on identifying the motivations behind your actions and consciously selecting ways to fulfil these needs positively. Develop a plan for implementing the activities you have identified. For example, if you feel the need for comfort is essential to you, establish a timetable of activities aligned with your beliefs and goals. Tracking your progress will allow you to adjust your approach as needed.

Reality Therapy and Choice Theory emphasise the impact of responsibility and choice on our behaviour patterns, highlighting the importance of recognising and addressing our underlying needs to guide us towards making thoughtful choices that can bring about meaningful change.

The Cognitive Behavioural Techniques (CBTs) a known treatment approach in psychology focuses on the connection, between thoughts, feelings and behaviours. It operates on the belief that our thoughts impact our emotions and behaviours and vice versa which guides its effectiveness. By identifying and challenging thoughts and beliefs CBTs assist individuals in enhancing their emotional responses and actions.

Why is CBT effective in achieving outcomes for individuals? CBTs provide tools to support individuals in overcoming undesirable habits and unconstructive thoughts. Through techniques such as restructuring and behavioural experiments CBTs assist individuals in developing healthier thinking patterns and coping strategies. This approach can be particularly beneficial, in addressing anxiety disorders depression and other mental health challenges.

One negative belief may be *"I lack the skills to succeed in my career or personal life situations"*. Being able to substitute the pessimism with a pragmatic and well-rounded viewpoint, like *"There are areas where I excel and others that I'm working on enhancing, as part of my ongoing growth."*

Remember when you faced and reevaluated your thoughts, how was it to find evidence that goes against those negative beliefs? What difference did it make in your feelings as you began to adopt a more balanced mindset? This exercise illustrates how Cognitive Behavioural Therapy (CBT) can assist in breaking free from thinking patterns and developing a more practical and hopeful outlook on life.

Regularly practice identifying and dealing with thoughts to seamlessly incorporate Cognitive Behavioural Therapy (CBT) into your daily routine. Keep a journal to track your thoughts emotions and behaviours and apply cognitive restructuring techniques to transform unhelpful thoughts. Over time this process can lead to improved health and a more balanced mindset.

CBT offers methods to modify negative thinking patterns and behaviours effectively by challenging and reframing unhelpful thoughts to develop healthier coping mechanisms and cognitive habits for improving emotional responses and behaviour.

Neuro Linguistic Programming (NLP) involves using language and communication to understand and influence behaviour by focusing on how language interacts with the brain and behaviour patterns to alter thoughts and emotions through changing perspectives and reactions to situations.

Why does NLP matter much in our lives today? NLP offers approaches to change negative beliefs and enhance how we communicate effectively to achieve personal and career goals. Incorporating methods, like anchoring and reframing can assist in moving unproductive habits and adopting more empowering approaches.

Select a behaviour or belief you want to change. Perhaps if speaking in front of people makes you nervous. Think back to a time when you felt anxious about it in the past. Create an anchor using NLP techniques, like a hand gesture or comforting word. That brings you a feeling of calm and confidence. Whenever you need a boost of self-assurance in similar situations, in the future use this anchor and observe how it impacts your actions and feelings.

Reflect on the impact of using the anchor on your behaviour and self-assurance levels in the past. Did it help you feel more secure and composed? Anchoring is a technique in NLP that can assist in attaining mental states and applying them effectively in challenging situations. By experimenting with these techniques over time you'll find the strategies that work best for you.

In situations where assistance is required to incorporate NLP techniques into your everyday routine establish and utilise anchors effectively. Experiment with approaches to discover the one that resonates with you the most. Consistent practice is key, to utilising these tools and integrating them into your behavioural repertoire.

Using Neuro Linguistic Programming (or NLP) provides methods for leveraging language and viewpoints to shift limiting thoughts and actions positively in various situations. By employing anchoring and reframing techniques effectively in your interactions and discussions with others, can enhance your communication skills significantly. NLP can also assist you in overcoming barriers to achieve your desired goals more smoothly.

By blending techniques with acupressure methods, in a practice known as Emotional Freedom Techniques (EFT) also called Tapping therapy aims to address negative emotions and issues by tapping on specific acupressure points on the body's energy system to alleviate emotional barriers and restore balance.

Why is EFT effective? EFT addresses trauma and anxiety well, as stress and other emotional issues that contribute to various problems people face in their lives. EFT reduces the intensity of feelings and promotes emotional recovery through tapping on acupressure points. Simple to incorporate into routines this adaptable method can be used to tackle a wide range of issues.

Find a spot where you can sit comfortably and relax your mind for a moment or two and focus on a specific feeling or issue, you'd like to address. Like stress or worry perhaps? EFT is a gentle process of touching key acupressure points on your body. Starting from the side of your hand to the crown of your head down to your eyebrows and around your eyes, ending at your collarbone area. As you gently tap on your body's energy points with your fingertips while softly reciting an affirmation, like *"Despite my worries and fears I fully embrace myself "* observe how your feelings evolve during the tapping session.

Remember how your mood shifted when you tried tapping technique before? Did you feel like your emotions were less intense? EFT can make it easier to handle stress and negative feelings by guiding you in recognising and letting go of obstacles in your way. Making EFT a regular part of your routine can empower you to cultivate emotional strength and overall happiness.

Consistently practicing tapping can assist you in integrating EFT into your self-care routine. Gradually progress to tackling complex emotional issues beginning with those that you feel confident of managing. Keep a journal to monitor your progress and note any changes in your emotions. Experiment, with tapping techniques and rhythms to discover which ones resonate best with you.

The EFT/Tapping approach is known to assist in dealing with issues and promoting healing processes effectively. By releasing emotions and restoring emotional balance through focusing on challenges and utilising specific acupressure points individuals can experience improved overall wellbeing and resilience.

Hypnosis is a technique that helps individuals access the subconscious mind for personal growth and change purposes. It involves inducing a state of relaxation where individuals can explore underlying issues and become more open to suggestions. This method can effectively address a range of concerns such as, anxiety disorders, phobias and maladaptive behaviours.

Why is hypnosis effective in helping individuals improve their wellbeing and behaviour patterns? Engaging in hypnosis allows individuals to delve into and potentially modify tendencies that could be impacting their emotions and actions. Collaborating with a certified hypnotherapist can assist individuals in identifying and addressing root issues effectively to pave the way for enduring growth and change.

When you reach a level of self-awareness and understanding yourself deeply as a person, on a profound level, beyond just superficial awareness of your subconscious tendencies—that's when you take the bold step to question and change them actively. Begin by documenting your thoughts and feelings alongside your actions over an extended period. As you observe these aspects closely in your life, log or journal entries day by day or week by week patterns will emerge. These recurring patterns will give you insights, into the underlying beliefs buried within your subconscious mind that influence the course of your life journey in ways you may not have realised before.

One key part of this process involves questioning the accuracy of your thoughts that come automatically to mind without conscious effort or control over them. For instance, if you often find yourself thinking *"I will never achieve success "* it's beneficial to pause and reflect on the basis of this thought. Is there evidence supporting it, or is it a skewed version of reality? By challenging these negative thoughts and examining the validity, behind them thoroughly, you can gradually diminish their influence and substitute them with more level-headed and beneficial alternatives. Engaging in this method is crucial in approaches such, as CBT that support individuals in overcoming thought patterns.

A crucial part of this process involves pinpointingng the core fears that fuel your behaviours. Ingrained patterns are commonly linked to profound fears, like the fear of being rejected or failing. By acknowledging these fears and concerns, you can address them head on, reducing their impact and the hold over how you behave.

Visualisation is vital in reshaping patterns effectively in various practices like Neuro Linguistic Programming (NLP) and hypnotherapy. By using visualisation techniques, in these approaches you get to visualise and change how you respond to situations. Then picturing yourself putting things off or feeling stressed out imagine yourself being self-assured and composed instead. This method aids in rewiring your brain which makes it simpler to incorporate these behaviours into your daily life.

Find a spot where you can sit or lie down and relax your body and mind by taking a deep breath with your eyes closed. Visualise yourself standing at the top of a staircase with ten steps leading down and imagine each step bringing you to a state of tranquillity. When you reach the bottom of the stairs in your mind's eye envisioning a secure setting where you feel completely at ease. In this state of mind focus, on a specific challenge or goal that you want to address and visualise yourself successfully achieving your goal or overcoming the obstacle. Take a moment to envision this victory before returning to your usual state of consciousness by ascending the stairs gently.

Reflect on your experience with the hypnosis exercise – how did your feelings and views towards the goal or issue shift, as you relaxed and visualised it all out in your mind's eye? By delving into your patterns and guiding you through them during hypnosis sessions, it can assist you in resolving issues that may have proven difficult to tackle through conventional methods.

Engaging with a hypnotherapist who guides you through personalised sessions can support your integration of hypnosis into your self-improvement endeavours effectively. Alternatively, you can reinforce changes through self-hypnosis techniques. Consistent dedication and perseverance, in applying this method will enable you to uncover and reshape seated subconscious patterns, however, this transformation process requires time to unfold fully.

Hypnosis can be a tool, for tapping into and reshaping subconscious patterns to facilitate personal growth and transformation. Engaging in relaxation techniques and visualisation exercises enables individuals to address issues and approach their goals with greater ease.

In this section we've explored methods of therapy and coaching designed to aid in changing behaviour and addressing unconscious habits. These approaches range from Choice Theory and Reality Therapy, to CBT, NLP, EFT and Hypnosis, each offering tools and tactics for personal growth and transformation. Understanding and applying these methods can assist in conquering challenges reprogramming the subconscious and achieving lasting change.

Choose one of the methods discussed in this chapter that resonates with you the most for your task. Incorporate this technique into your routine. For example, with CBT you could maintain a thought journal to track and challenge thoughts. If you opt for EFT establish a tapping routine. Write down your plan and set goals, for implementing the chosen approach.

When reflecting on the method you prefer and how you plan to incorporate it into your project's framework. What are your goals with this strategy and what outcomes are you striving to achieve through its implementation? How do you plan to keep track of your progress and evaluate its effectiveness along the way? Consider any obstacles you might encounter and devise strategies to overcome them as part of your planning process.

Stay patient and persistent as you begin implementing your chosen approach as progress doesn't happen overnight and challenges are bound to come up along the way. Stay committed to your tasks. Be open, to adjusting your tactics when needed. Celebrate every small step of progress you make no matter how minor it may seem.

Therapy and coaching provide a range of approaches to tackling subconscious habits and encouraging behavioural shifts for personal growth and self-improvement journey. You can explore techniques like Choice Theory and practices such as CBT (Cognitive Behavioural Therapy) NLP (Neuro Linguistic Programming) EFT (Emotional Freedom Technique) and Hypnotherapy to empower yourself towards personal progress and transformation. Embrace these tools as part of your path to self-improvement. Continue with determination and a strong will to advance further in your personal growth journey.

Summary & Practice

Building blocks of self-awareness, like laying the foundation brick by brick. Unconscious emotions and thoughts can have an impact on your actions without you even realising it.

- Explore the recurring ideas in your emotions and behaviours to understand yourself better.
- Keep a journal to monitor these trends and understand what triggers them.
- Practice mindfulness exercises to observe your thoughts without judging them in any way.
- Use techniques of visualisation to map out the links between your thoughts and feelings and how they influence your actions.
- Discover the underlying motivations behind your actions.
- Explore positive ways to meet those needs authentically.
- Put Transformation into Practice.
- Remember to take notes on your thoughts and emotions to track any recurring patterns in your actions.
- Question the validity of challenging thoughts.
- Replace them with more balanced alternatives.

- Uncover the anxieties that shape your behaviours and experiment with imagining responses in familiar scenarios you are familiar with.

Incorporating these habits into your routine can help you better understand your inner thoughts and bring about positive changes in how you think and act and in your emotional state too! Keep in mind that change doesn't happen overnight, it requires dedication and perseverance— stick with it and you'll see progress, over time.

Chapter 4

Intuition

The intention of Chapter 4 – Intuition, is to create a powerful shift in how you make decisions by encouraging you to rely on your wisdom instead of just logic alone. It prompts you to go beyond logic and listen to your intuition. The kind that comes from deep within your subconscious and past experiences. When you blend this insight with rational thinking, in decision making processes you'll adopt a more comprehensive approach that resonates with what you aim for in life. The aim is to help you tap into both your thinking and intuition to change your ingrained habits and make meaningful long-term improvements, in your life.

Have you ever thought about how relying on your gut feeling could be as crucial as using methods to shift your subconscious beliefs? Picture being able to make decisions and predict results not through reasoning but also by connecting with an inner wisdom that instinctively leads you towards your aspirations. In this section of the book, we delve into how being mindful of strategies at play and trusting your intuition can significantly boost your capacity to bring about enduring transformations in your conditioning.

Start by becoming more aware of how your gut feelings and inner nudges impact the choices you make in life of solely relying on logic for decision making purposes. By being mindful of the way these intuitive sensations emerge within you and recognising the recurring patterns in your decision-making journey, it can assist you in navigating situations by balancing both rationality and instinctive responses.

Think back to a choice you made following your instinct or gut reaction. Take a moment to visualise that situation with your eyes shut. What feelings or sensations did you feel at that point in time? How did they sway your decision-making process? Reflect on what might have occurred if you had solely relied on logic to make the same decision, without considering your intuition. How could the result have diverged in this scenario?

Reflecting on your instincts helps you grasp how your subconscious tendencies influence your behaviours significantly. Intuition may seem enigmatic at times, it is actually based on keen pattern recognition of different life experiences and subtle subconscious signals. Taking note of your instincts, blending them with rational thought can enhance your ability to make decisions effectively.

Feeling like a puzzle most of the time intuitive judgment is that gut feeling or inner sense guiding your choices and actions. What if we could systematically understand and harness this skill? By blending strategies with intuitive judgment you can navigate challenging situations, with more finesse and align your subconscious mind with your goals.

Think about a decision you made recently that was mostly influenced by your gut feeling or intuition without overthinking it much. Close your eyes. Recall the moment when you had to make that choice. Visualise the scenario in your mind – the situation itself, along with the emotions you felt at that moment and how things turned out in the end. Looking back at it now –

reflect on how much of your decision was guided by your intuition and how that might have impacted the outcome.

Imagine deciding solely relying on analysis and logic without considering your instincts or gut feelings as a factor in the choice making process. How might this alternative strategy vary from the decision you would typically make? Take some time to reflect on how your intuition guided you and how it contrasted with a rational approach.

Remember how your intuition influenced your decision-making process in the past and reflect on any patterns or insights you discovered about how your intuitive judgments align with or differ from analysis. Doesn't it seem like intuitive judgments often aid and enhance decision making through subtle pattern recognition and accumulated experience?

As you delve into grasping judgment more deeply you will start to notice the significance of pattern recognition in it. Your subconscious mind is always at work processing information recognising repeated themes and structures in your surroundings. This is the mechanism through which intuition operates—it picks up on patterns drawn from experiences and subtly guides your decisions. For instance you may have a gut feeling that something is not quite right in a conversation or that a particular choice feels like the correct one even when lacking all the logical evidence to support it.

Understanding the importance of recognising patterns is key in making decisions. Whether they are intuitive or logical ones in various aspects of life and work scenarios alike. Through identifying patterns that emerge from experiences enabling you to anticipate potential results effectively. This skill serves as an asset in managing obstacles, with more foresight and assurance both personally and professionally.

Think about a situation that keeps happening in your life – it could be a problem you often deal with such as managing your time or a good opportunity that keeps coming up. Write down times when this situation has occurred before. What similarities do you notice among these instances. How have your reactions affected the results?

Through examining these recurring patterns in your life experiences and actions, you can start to grasp how your innermost thoughts shape the way you act and make choices without even realising it yourself. This level of self-awareness empowers you to tune your responses with greater foresight moving forward, by blending gut feelings with rational thinking to steer your course.

Understanding the role of judgment can help you blend it with logical thinking to achieve improved outcomes allowing you to leverage cognitive evaluation and intuitive insights for making wiser choices.

Engage with your feelings and blend them with rational thought to utilise your intuition effectively when making judgments. Pause to ponder your instinctive responses in light of the available information. This holistic approach may enhance your decision-making skills and lead to wiser choices.

When paired with methods and relying on intuition, decision making can be a powerful way to shift ingrained beliefs and achieve your goals successfully. Embracing and trusting your intuition enables you to make decisions and align your subconscious thoughts with your desired outcomes.

One fundamental aspect of judgment involves recognising patterns in your surroundings and experiences. Identifying common themes and structures that occur regularly. This ability to recognise patterns allows your subconscious mind to anticipate outcomes and guide your decision-making process.

Why is it important to focus on recognising patterns in situations and contexts you might wonder? Recognising patterns enables individuals to comprehend information and predict potential outcomes by drawing on previous experiences. It allows for navigation of challenges and opportunities, through the application of instinctual comprehension. Enhancing one's ability to recognise patterns can lead to improved decision making and informed judgments.

Think about a recurring pattern in your life. A challenge you often encounter or an opportunity that comes up repeatedly for you to seize on. This could be struggling with managing your time or facing obstacles in your work environment on a regular basis. Take some time to reflect on this pattern and make notes of instances when you have experienced it.

Examine the underlying reasons for this pattern. Identify the common factors at play here. How have your responses to these situations influenced the outcomes? Use this analysis to learn how you can better manage or leverage this trend in the future.

Consider reflecting on the patterns you discovered and the insights you uncovered in the process how do you think being aware of these patterns could influence your actions and choices moving forward? Recognising and pinpointing recurring patterns can assist in making decisions and predicting potential outcomes based on previous encounters.

Be sure to jot down recurring themes and life situations in a notebook to enhance your ability to recognise patterns better. Regularly analyse these patterns to identify trends and insights. This understanding can aid you in developing strategies for incorporating or dealing with these patterns when making decisions.

Intuitive judgment relies heavily on pattern recognition to anticipate outcomes and steer your decisions effectively

Enhancing your ability to identify and interpret recurring patterns can leverage your understanding for improved decision making and lasting personal growth.

Having awareness means being able to anticipate and prepare for future events by relying on your instincts and recognising patterns in advance. Creating strategies to achieve your goals involves blending your intuitive thoughts with logical reasoning.

Understanding the importance of strategy is crucial as it enables you to navigate through situations with foresight and align your actions with future objectives effectively. Integrating planning with intuitive decision making allows you to develop actionable plans by leveraging subconscious insights leading to positive outcomes in various scenarios.

Consider a goal you aim to achieve in the short, medium or long term. Whether it's nurturing your relationships or progressing in your career or business ventures. Reflect on the obstacles and potential challenges that may arise along the way. Drawing from your understanding of patterns and trends in your life experiences and surroundings can help you identify opportunities or recurring obstacles related to this goal.

Craft a blueprint by blending logical analysis with your innate intuition. Outline specific actions you can take to leverage opportunities and tackle obstacles. Consider how your strategic decision making could benefit from thoughts and inspirations.

Reflect on how integrating planning with intuitive decision making altered your approach to achieving your goals. Did this fusion of methods bring forth novel ideas or perspectives? Strategic mindfulness enables you to craft pragmatic plans aligned with inner intuitions and enhance your ability to attain your goals.

Incorporate your gut feelings with thinking when making decisions to enhance your strategic awareness effectively and a purposeful growth strategy evolves by regularly revisiting and adjusting your plans based on new insights and information. Anticipate challenges and opportunities by leveraging your ability to recognise patterns then adapt your strategy accordingly.

Having a mindset strategy allows you to blend logical strategising with gut instincts to achieve your long-term objectives effectively and efficiently. Creating plans driven by your inner intuitions can assist you in navigating challenging situations with greater ease and aligning your actions with desired outcomes.

Deep analysis involves assessing outcomes based on an understanding of the factors influencing a situation. To make better decisions you need to blend your intuition with diligent research and predictions.

Understanding the significance of analysis is crucial as it allows you to anticipate and prepare for potential outcomes based on a detailed examination of relevant factors, combining in depth analysis with straightforward observations, can assist in developing more effective strategies to achieve your goals and generate precise predictions.

Consider a goal or decision that involves multiple factors and potential outcomes—perhaps a substantial financial investment or a career change in mind. Leverage your ability to recognise patterns by gathering information on variables and identifying trends and potential consequences.

Take a look at these factors and balance factual information with gut feelings to craft a comprehensive plan that considers both risks and opportunities fully. Reflect on how your detailed analysis method influenced your choices and align it with your actions.

Reflect on how your thought process evolved when you integrated analysis with intuitive judgment. Did the in-depth examination and basic observations spark insights or solutions for you? Deep analysis merges scrutiny with unconscious intuition to enhance your ability to make well informed choices.

Enhance your decision-making skills by combining intuition and rational analysis to improve your ability to make calculations effectively. Regularly refine your ideas based on new information and insights. Predict outcomes through pattern recognition and adapt your strategies accordingly.

Incorporating analysis and predictions alongside intuitive judgment enhances your decision-making process enabling you to formulate more effective strategies for achieving your goals and generating precise forecasts.

When making decisions based on intuition at a deep level of understanding and insightfulness, it is crucial to not just acknowledge the patterns guiding your choices but also leverage them to influence your future results effectively. This requires blending knowledge and thorough analysis with intuitive perceptions. Strategic awareness enables you to anticipate obstacles and possibilities in line with your overarching objectives. Delving into assessment means carefully weighing the different elements involved by harmonising gut feelings with logical reasoning.

Start by selecting an objective you are striving for at present. Whether it involves progressing in your profession or enhancing your connections and actively seeking personal development opportunities. Reflect on the obstacles and chances that may emerge as you progress towards it. Resolve to employ your ability to recognise patterns to spot threads related to this aspiration. Are there any incidents that could guide your present approach?

Let's start by crafting a strategy that blends analytical thinking with gut instinctive reasoning. Outline concrete actions to tackle obstacles and maximise chances for success. How can your gut feelings aid in making choices? In crafting this strategy account for how thorough analysis—assessing both the dangers and rewards—can enhance your decision-making approach.

Thinking about how mixing gut feelings with insight, has shaped how you pursue your goal and has been quite impactful for me too! Have you found yourself seeing things from an angle by blending these methods together in your approach to problem solving and decision making at a higher level now? You're not just depending on reasoning or instinct anymore—now it's all about harnessing both to craft a more holistic and efficient plan for achieving success.

In this section of the discussion we explored the concept of decision making and how a thoughtful analysis, strategic understanding and pattern perception could enhance it. By blending these methods, you can incorporate thoughts and unconscious observations to bring about enduring transformations in your minds subconscious programming.

Think about an objective or choice you're focusing your efforts towards as your final task for the day's session. Utilise the tactics discussed in this section—recognising patterns and strategies strategically and delving into calculations—to develop a comprehensive plan of action. Reflect upon how these approaches align with your gut instincts and influence the choices you make.

Reflect on how employing these methods influenced your goals or outcomes in the past. How did incorporating analysis alongside intuitive reasoning provide you with fresh insights? Which of these techniques played a role in shaping your choices and organising your plans? Consider how you could continue applying these methods to steer your decisions and goals.

Make sure you regularly review and adjust your plans based on ideas and experiences as you work on enhancing your intuition and decision-making skills steadily over time. To enhance your ability to achieve your goals effectively incorporate insights and patterns recognition along with careful analysis, into your decision-making routine.

By relying on your gut instinct and analytical skills, while tapping into your understanding of things can significantly boost your ability to reprogram your subconscious mind effectively for lasting outcomes. When you blend these methods together you can enhance your decision-making skills in challenging situations. Align your unconscious thoughts with your desired outcomes. View these strategies as resources on your path to success and self-improvement.

Summary & Practice

Establishing the fundamentals of intuition. When you're faced with choices or decisions to make it is crucial to combine your gut feelings with thinking for a balanced perspective. Using pattern recognition to predict outcomes based on experiences is a valuable approach in decision making.

- Remember to think about how your instinct influences the decisions you make.
- Reflect on the decisions you've relied on your gut feelings for and assess their outcomes in hindsight.
- Improve skills by identifying patterns.
- Improve your ability to recognise recurring trends in your experiences.
- Consider how these patterns influence the decisions you make and the actions you take.
- Grasping ideas and delving into examination.
- Combine your intuition with thinking to ensure that your choices align with your overarching goals and aspirations.
- Draw on analysis to consider the advantages and

disadvantages of your decisions by combining intuition with logic.

Reflect about how intuition, recognising patterns, and being strategic will play an essential role in reaching your goals. By integrating these practices into your daily life you can rely on both gut feelings and logic to guide your decisions. This balance will help you make lasting changes in your subconscious habits allowing you to achieve your goals with increased ease and confidence.

Chapter 5

Patterns & Strategies

The intention of Chapter 5 - Patterns & Strategies, is to create a powerful transformation in how you approach life by recognising and intentionally shaping the patterns that influence your decisions. This chapter encourages you to notice the themes in your thoughts and actions and to devise approaches that support your objectives. By merging understanding with pattern identification skills, you acquire the power to purposefully steer your behaviours and results towards your desired outcomes. The main goal is to help you to liberate yourself from ingrained routines, and intentionally shape your life in a way that leads to enduring transformations, that resonate with your dreams and goals.

What if you could unlock the power of your mind not just by adjusting thoughts and beliefs but also by tapping into strategic wisdom and recognising patterns effectively? Picture yourself identifying and creating patterns in your life experiences that resonate with your dreams and ambitions, thereby reshaping your journey in a new way. This section delves into reshaping the mind by leveraging strategic insights and recognising patterns to initiate purposeful and significant changes.

In embarking on this journey of self-discovery and growth it is crucial to cultivate an awareness of the recurring patterns that influence our actions and choices in life. Like a skilled chess player who recognises winning strategies through patterns on the board, our subconscious also operates on patterns that can either propel us forward or hold us back. The initial step involves observing how certain behaviours or thought processes manifest repeatedly across areas of our lives. By acknowledging these patterns that emerge consistently, we gain insight into how our subconscious mind impacts the decisions we make.

Think about a goal or challenge you faced and reflect on the actions you took to deal with it. Firstly, you should close your eyes. Ponder if your problem-solving approach followed a usual pattern. Do you have strategies or habits that you typically utilise in similar scenarios? Jot down any recurring patterns or themes that spring to mind.

When you notice these recurring themes and behaviours in your life you begin to understand how your instincts influence the way you behave. This realisation forms the basis for developing plans that match your objectives. Keeping a journal of your experiences and choices enables you to monitor these trends giving you the chance to identify which approaches bring about outcomes and which ones might require tweaking.

Consider the story of a chess player who recognises and anticipates patterns that pave the way for victory instead of just reacting to immediate dangers in a game scenario. Similarly in life we have the ability to positively impact our lives by understanding and shaping the patterns within our subconscious mind. This section aims to guide you in mastering these concepts and facilitating lasting change in your life accordingly.

Recall a situation where you faced a challenge or task and think about the steps you took to address it. Consider how your problem-solving approach in situations may reveal a consistent pattern in your actions. Take a moment to reflect on whether certain guiding principles or decisions tend to emerge in similar circumstances.

Please jot down any elements or patterns that catch your attention. How have these trends impacted your outcomes. In what manner? These recurring themes might offer insights that could shape your choices or plans.

Remember to reflect on your notes and consider why certain habits or methods consistently appear in your decision-making process. Do you notice any recurring patterns or insights that could influence how you approach challenges? Understanding these trends can assist you in developing practical strategies to achieve your goals.

Begin by writing down your experiences and decisions to enhance your ability to recognise patterns and develop awareness effectively. Regularly revisit this journal to identify recurring themes and strategies that you can use to devise approaches aligned with your goals and beliefs. By implementing these concepts into your planning process you can enhance your effectiveness in achieving the outcomes you desire.

Two powerful techniques to understand your mind involve being observant and recognising patterns effectively. Finding and creating successful patterns can aid in shaping your approach to challenges and goals leading to more intentional and impactful transformations in your life.

As you get better at spotting trends in your actions and thoughts patterns, it is essential to delve into how these patterns impact the choices you make. Recognising patterns can be an asset as it enables you to foresee potential results by drawing on past encounters. For example, if you notice that certain behaviours or ways of thinking always lead to outcomes in your personal or work life by recognising these trends you can start to anticipate how forthcoming decisions will play out.

Why is this significant? Noticing patterns enables you to identify opportunities and obstacles before they fully emerge providing you with the insight to adapt your approach accordingly. Consider a scenario from your life where you have faced repeated challenges— in your job or personal relationships. Jot down these occurrences. Pinpoint any similar aspects or familiar methods.

Now take a moment to think about how these trends have shaped your choices and results far in life. Do you notice any habits that you tend to follow in such scenarios? How could modifying these habits potentially change the outcomes? By examining these trends, you can begin crafting plans that enable you to make wiser decisions going forward.

Recognising patterns is essential when it comes to reshaping your mind's programming. Identifying and changing patterns that are no longer beneficial to you, will bring about the opportunity to introduce new ones, that are in line with your goals and aspirations.

Recognising patterns in your life involves identifying and understanding recurring themes and trends that occur regularly. The capacity to do so is beneficial, for anticipating outcomes based on past actions—a crucial aspect of rewiring the subconscious mind.

Why is recognising patterns important in everyday life decisions and actions and how does it impact the outcomes you achieve and the choices you make moving forward? Recognising these recurring themes and tendencies can guide you in shaping strategies that align with your goals and enable you to make informed decisions.

Select an aspect of your life, like your career or personal connections. Where you have faced recurring challenges or situations repeatedly encountered in that domain of your life. Take note of any recurring themes or consistencies you have observed in this realm of experience. For example, you may often encounter hurdles at work. Confront similar issues within your relationships on a regular basis.

Investigate these patterns to find factors or reasons behind these repeated occurrences. Evaluate how these inclinations have influenced your decisions and outcomes and consider if altering these behaviours could lead to favourable results.

Reflect on the trends and patterns you observed in the past. How do these trends influence your outlook on opportunities and obstacles? Have you gained any insights into how these behaviours impact your outcomes? By leveraging the information and analysis of these trends, one can develop effective strategies and steer future choices.

Make it a habit to reflect on your experiences and decisions regularly to identify recurring themes and enhance your ability to recognise patterns effectively. This insight will empower you to develop strategies that capitalise on opportunities or address common challenges you encounter. By understanding and adapting these tendencies you can better navigate towards your goals with progression in mind.

Master your subconscious by honing your knack for spotting patterns. Keep an eye out for those trends in your day-to-day happenings, to ace your game plan and make sound choices that align with your goals.

Having this knowledge means being able to predict and plan for future events by analysing information and gaining insights to come up with practical solutions to achieve your goals.

Strategic insight is essential because it enables you to navigate situations proactively and align your actions with future aspirations. By integrating your insights with strategic thinking, you can devise effective plans to enhance your ability to achieve goals and reshape your mindset subconsciously.

Consider a goal you aim to achieve in the short, medium, or long term. Whether it is building stronger relationships, progressing in your career path or some other goal you have in mind. Reflect on the situation and the potential obstacles or opportunities you may encounter along the way. Draw on your ability to recognise patterns to identify any recurring challenges or possibilities related to this objective.

Craft a strategy that accounts for potential hurdles and incorporates your insights. Outline specific actions you could take to capitalise on opportunities and overcome barriers. Consider how your strategic thinking could enhance your tactics in achieving your goal.

Remember how your way of achieving your goal shifted when you integrated understanding with your talent for spotting patterns in things around you? Did this blend of tactics spark thoughts or perspectives for you? Being attuned to strategy enables you to craft strategies rooted in your observations that align with your ability to achieve your goals.

Enhance your awareness by integrating your insights into pattern recognition with thoughtful planning techniques, allowing for continuous growth and adaptation in response to new information and experiences. Stay proactive in reviewing and adjusting your strategies based on updated data and personal observations to effectively anticipate and address challenges and opportunities.

When you merge your knack for spotting patterns with planning, it enables you to achieve your long-range goals by applying strategic thinking skills effectively. Combining these methods enables you to develop realistic strategies tailored to your objectives and enhance your ability to navigate challenging situations more effectively.

At the level of expertise and skilfulness, you are not just identifying patterns but actively shaping them to fit your future objectives This approach requires blending strategic insight with pattern detection in order to establish a blueprint for achievement. Strategic insight empowers you to anticipate potential obstacles and openings, while pattern recognition aids in comprehending how your previous encounters can guide your forthcoming decisions

Start by reflecting on a goal you are aiming for in the long term. It could be related to your career path or personal development goals or even your relationships with others in your life. Think about the patterns you have noticed along the way and how they might either propel you forward or hold you back in achieving your goal. Create a well-thought-through plan that tackles any challenges that might come your way and takes advantage of any opportunities that arise. Be sure to outline actions you can take to keep yourself on course and be willing to adjust your approach as necessary.

Understanding the picture extends beyond mere planning, it includes consistently assessing and adjusting your strategy in response to fresh perspectives that arise along the way to achieving your objective goal. Take a moment to contemplate how your tendencies shape your choices as you progress forward. Are you reverting to familiar routines or actively cultivating new behaviours that are in line with your desired outcomes?

By blending mindfulness with recognising patterns effectively, you establish a robust structure for rewiring your subconscious thoughts. This method helps you transcend reactive choices and seize command over the patterns that influence your existence.

Creating patterns involves constructing structures and approaches that align with your goals and principles while developing strategies that effectively guide your actions and choices relies on utilising strategic insight and recognising patterns.

Why is it important to create patterns in your life design process? You can shape patterns that align with your goals and have an impact on your outcomes and experiences in a certain way. Crafting effective patterns allows you to reshape your unconscious thoughts and align your actions with the desired outcomes

In your life, think of a goal or aspiration—such as achieving a career milestone or improving your well-being—and devise a plan to establish routines that support this goal effectively, by creating intentional strategies and actionable plans tailored to your objective.

If your goal is to improve your health and well-being aspect by aspect – consider establishing a routine that consists of regular physical activity sessions and balanced nutrition coupled with mindfulness practices in mind. Contemplate how these established routines could support you in achieving your desired goals and enhance your ability to do effectively.

Reflect on how your approach to achieving your goals shifted based on the pattern you encountered. Did you find that intentionally incorporating structures and methods assisted in aligning your actions with your objective? Developing patterns enables you to steer your conduct and choices, which influence your outcomes and experiences.

Start by crafting strategies after clearly defining your goals and anticipated outcomes first and foremost. Establish frameworks and strategies to propel these objectives forward. Regularly. Adjust your strategies based on your progress and learnings. Tailoring strategies to align with your goals can aid in reshaping your mind and enhancing your ability to achieve the intended outcomes.

Harnessing the power of your subconscious and achieving your goals is made easier with the aid of crafting patterns that align with your objectives. Creating structures and strategies tailored to your aspirations will empower you to steer your behaviours and choices effectively, leading to impactful and enduring transformations.

In this chapter, we highlighted the importance of tapping into the mind by exploring strategic comprehension concepts and effectively recognising patterns. Discovering and building patterns can enhance your decision-making skills, align your actions with your goals and lead to enduring changes in your life.

For your task today, think about a current goal or challenge you are facing in your life and apply the techniques discussed in this chapter. Recognising patterns, strategic planning and pattern design. To craft a comprehensive plan of action that considers how these methods can help you achieve your goals and structure your approach.

Reflecting on employing these methods to achieve your goal or address a challenge, what kind of insights did you gain from combining expertise with recognising patterns? How did the act of crafting patterns influence your approach and outcomes? Consider how you could continue utilising these tactics in ventures and challenges.

Make sure to reassess and adjust your strategies based on new understandings and lessons learned as you enhance your strategic understanding and ability to recognise patterns effectively. Develop patterns that align with your goals and enhance your ability to achieve desired outcomes.

Taping into your mind and achieving lasting change requires understanding your surroundings and recognising patterns effectively. By merging these tactics, you can establish intentional routines that guide your actions and choices to yield better outcomes. Embrace these approaches as aids in your journey towards success and self-improvement.

Summary & Practice

Remember to consider your tendencies when behaving and deciding on things. Think about how your past experiences influence the decisions you are making now.

- Consider reflecting upon your goals or challenges and note any common patterns or strategies that have caught your attention.
- Don't forget to keep a diary to track these patterns and how they affect your outcomes.
- Improving Your Strategic Comprehension.
- Use pattern recognition to anticipate challenges and benefits.
- Explore the impact of altering behaviours on the outcomes achieved.
- Formulating plans to attain success.
- Incorporate knowledge of tactics and the aptitude to recognise trends to formulate a long-term strategy.
- Remember to review and update your plan based on insights and experiences gained along the way.
- Create designs that align with your goals to transform your mindset for success.

By incorporating these methods into your routine, you can utilise the benefits of recognising patterns and being more aware strategically to steer your choices and actions with greater purpose. This method will assist you in harmonising your thoughts with your defined objectives resulting in enduring and significant changes.

Chapter 6

Depth Calculation

The intention of Chapter 6 - Depth Calculation, is to help you elevate your transformation by exploring the depths of your thoughts and uncovering the underlying motivations behind your actions more profoundly than before. This chapter encourages you to look beyond insights and cultivate the skill to accurately gauge the intensity of your feelings as well as understand your fears and convictions in detail. By unveiling and dealing with these factors that shape you from within, you can tap into the potential to make enduring transformations in your life. The aim is to help you turn your acquired understanding into concrete steps that match your everyday routines with your inner desires, for personal development and achievement.

Picture yourself delving into your thoughts to reveal the underlying forces that impact your choices and behaviours hidden from plain view. Wouldn't that be fascinating? Consider if you had the ability to meticulously gauge the intricacies of your drives, doubts and dreams with the precision of a researcher studying intricate systems. The key to unlocking your potential lies in mastering the technique known as depth calculation, a powerful tool enabling you to grasp and alter the core influencers moulding your existence.

When delving into the depths of your thoughts and feelings it is crucial to develop self-awareness and acknowledge that superficial thoughts and emotions may conceal deeper impacts on you as a person. It is similar to an explorer venturing into the ocean depths to uncover both valuable gems and potential risks. Understanding your subconscious calls for a similar voyage of discovery. Start by examining your thoughts and behaviours closely, then delve into the reasons driving them. Are these behaviours motivated by wants or do they originate from fundamental convictions or anxieties?

Start by selecting an aspect of your life that you'd like to understand better or make adjustments to it. Take a moment to shut your eyes and envision yourself delving into the depths of your thoughts and feelings hidden in your subconscious mind. While you delve deeper into this space within you where thoughts and emotions intertwine intricately with each other, reflect on any newfound revelations or insights that may come to light. Observe the emotions and beliefs that emerge as you navigate through this terrain. Jot down any recurring patterns or emotions that appear to influence the choices you make in this area of your life.

Think about these ideas for a moment. Have you discovered any aspects yet that were hidden from your view before now? Are there any fears or beliefs that are silently shaping how you act, that you hadn't thought about before? By recognising these layers of your thoughts and emotions more deeply, you will better understand what motivates your behaviours and use this insight to develop deliberate plans for making positive changes in your life.

Picture yourself as a deep-sea explorer diving into unexplored ocean depths, discovering hidden treasures and potential risks while mapping the terrain and gauging the depth with sophisticated equipment. Likewise, delving into the realm of depth computation can be likened to a journey that enables you to delve into the layers of your own subconscious mind and reveal valuable insights and patterns that have the potential to drive substantial personal growth.

Imagine yourself as a deep-sea explorer equipped to delve into the ocean depths and measure their mysteries. As you descend into the depths of your thoughts and emotions, like a diver exploring uncharted waters, you encounter layers that reveal different aspects of your thoughts, emotions and behaviours. While navigating through these layers, focus your attention on an aspect of your life where you seek transformation or understanding.

Take note of any discoveries or realisations as you navigate through these depths of thought and reflection. Pay attention to any emotions or thoughts that arise during this process. How does your current viewpoint on the issue align with these revelations? Have you encountered any perspectives or ideas in the process?

Reflect on your goals. The insights gained from the exercise. Why did certain traits of yours come to light? These observations reveal the factors influencing your actions and decisions. Understanding the depths of your subconscious can assist in addressing the root causes of your issues and devising practical strategies for growth.

To begin your journey towards transformation and understanding in an aspect of your life, you would need to pinpoint an area where you seek clarity or change for a deeper exploration within yourself. Delve into the layers of your subconscious through practices like introspection journaling or guided visualisation. Uncovering and comprehending these root causes can empower you to develop targeted strategies for addressing core issues and fostering lasting transformations.

Understanding and harnessing the power of your mind relies greatly on delving deep into its depths for insight and transformation that can bring about profound and enduring change in your life journey. Explore the underlying layers of your thoughts and emotions to uncover influences shaping your path and guide your personal growth.

When delving into the concept of measuring depth accuracy in your studies, it is important to go beyond just scratching the surface and delve into analysing the multiple layers that impact your actions. Exploring depth measurement enables you to understand the connections between your thoughts, feelings and previous encounters. This approach lets you unveil the hidden patterns that have been shaping your decisions without you realising it.

Why is determining depth in understanding things better? It allows for an examination of the root reasons behind your obstacles or ambitions. By delving deeper into your innermost thoughts and feelings hidden beneath the surface layers of consciousness, to uncover concealed fears or lingering emotions that might impede your progress forward. Once these are brought to light you can then address them head on, resulting in more profound and enduring transformations.

Think about a problem or obstacle you're dealing with in your life for a while now, and jot down some questions that can delve into the root of this issue further. For instance, *"What fears or beliefs might be fuelling this difficulty?". "In what ways are my previous experiences shaping how I act today?"* Utilise these questions to lead a writing session or meditation practice. Keep an eye out for any new perspectives or realisations that surface during this introspective exercise.

As you delve into these layers further down the line of thoughtfulness and reflection, take note of any repetitive sequences or overarching ideas that come to light naturally in this process of introspection and analysis. Consider what insights have been brought to your attention regarding the fundamental reasons behind your actions and reactions. By gaining a comprehension of these profound motivating factors that lie beneath the surface of your conscious awareness and drive your behaviour patterns – you can craft specific approaches tailored to tackle the core origins of the issue in question rather than merely addressing its outward manifestations.

Exploring your subconscious on a level involves delving into the underlying factors that influence your thoughts and emotions significantly. This process includes self-reflection exercises, like journaling or guided visualisation to gain an understanding of the root causes behind your challenges and goals.

Why delve into the depths of computation you may ask yourself? Well, it provides a framework to explore the interplay of internal components that shape your choices and actions in life. Grasping these influences can assist you in uncovering the root causes of your challenges enabling you to craft more effective strategies to achieve your goals successfully.

Choose any issue or challenge you're facing in your life. Create a set of questions to help you explore the deeper aspects of this problem. For example, *"What fears or beliefs may be playing a role in this situation?". "How are my past experiences shaping the way I behave now?"*

These prompts are designed to help you delve into the workings of your mind by engaging in reflective activities or writing in a journal. Pay close attention to any insights or recurring themes that arise and think about how they can influence your problem-solving approach. This method fosters self-reflection and enables you to gain a deeper understanding of your own subconscious thoughts.

Reflect on how you have navigated through the layers of your struggles in the past. How can exploring these depths lead to perspectives or insights? Have you uncovered any root causes that were previously unknown? Understanding these impacts enables you to craft targeted strategies, for change and address the core issues behind your challenges.

To effectively utilise depth measurements in your analysis process, engage in exploring the recesses of your subconscious thoughts. Utilise exercises, journaling or guided imagery to unearth the underlying reasons behind your actions and choices. Grasping these elements will aid you in devising strategies, for achieving your goals and overcoming challenges.

To truly understand and alter the core factors that shape your actions and decisions consider delving into the depths of your mind through introspection and reflection techniques that offer valuable insights and facilitate strategic goal setting, for enduring personal growth and achievement.

The core of delving into depth involves leveraging your understanding to formulate strategies and steps to tackle the root issues you have identified. This method requires you to integrate your knowledge of the workings of your subconscious mind with practical actions that align with your goals. For example, If you have realised that a fear of failure is hindering your progress, an actionable step could involve setting attainable objectives to boost your self-assurance.

What is the benefit of applying practicality in your approach to situations or challenges you encounter in life? Practicing practicality empowers you to translate your observations into actions that drive real change forward. By leveraging your understanding of the underlying factors influencing your behaviour you can craft targeted strategies that tackle the root causes of your issues and propel you towards achieving your desired outcomes.

Develop a plan of action rooted in a specific realisation or knowledge acquired from previous deep reflection exercises. In case you've discovered that previous trauma is impacting your actions you could devise a plan that involves seeking support resolving emotional issues and building new coping mechanisms.

When delving into the depths of your mind at a level of understanding oneself means more than just unveiling buried aspects of your thoughts. It also means translating them into practical steps, for personal growth and transformation. The crucial step here is to leverage the wisdom acquired from exploring the depths of your mind and use it to devise action plans that resonate with your aspirations. This journey entails merging your self-awareness with purposeful actions aimed at tackling the underlying issues triggering your obstacles.

For instance, suppose you find out from reflecting that your fear of failure right now is greatly impacted by past instances of rejection you faced before. If you've pinpointed this seated fear within yourself the next thing to do is come up with a strategy that enables you to face and defeat it head on. This could mean reaching out for help masterminding ways to handle the situation or participating in activities that progressively boost your self-assurance.

Create a plan of action that tackles the main problems you have identified and then lay out precise actions you could implement to include these findings in your everyday routine, considering how to seamlessly integrate these fresh approaches into your daily schedule and how you will track your development as time goes by.

By translating your understanding into steps you will start observing tangible shifts in your behaviour and decision-making process over time. Take a moment to consider the impact that utilising your insights has had on the way you tackle challenges or pursue goals. What changes have become apparent in your actions or results because of this approach? This practice of integrating awareness into practical steps is the key driver of individual development and enduring change.

Implement a feasible strategy based on your understanding of the situation at hand. How did putting your expertise into practice influence your outlook on the issue? Did implementing these insights lead to any adjustments, in how you act or the outcomes? Applying what you know in real life scenarios allows you to turn your knowledge into tasks that help your goals and foster personal growth.

Develop a strategy outlining the steps you will take to address the main issues encountered in effectively utilising the insights from your depth calculations analysis. Regularly review and modify your strategy based on your progress and any new ideas that arise. Transform your understanding into actionable steps to aid in your progress and facilitate substantial improvements.

To create lasting change and grow personally over time requires utilising insights into factors and taking practical steps forward based on that understanding. There is power in aligning your awareness of what drives your actions with targeted strategies to address challenges and make meaningful progress towards your goals. Implement this approach to turn your thoughts into actionable strategies that propel you towards achievement.

In this section we explored the concept of calculating depth and its potential in understanding the mind better. Exploring the layers of our thoughts and emotions can lead us to discover the core factors shaping our experiences and develop clear strategies for change.

Choose a challenge or objective in your life and apply the techniques for delving deep, discussed in this chapter as a final activity. Uncover hidden motivations by delving into the recesses of your subconscious mind and then devise a practical plan of action rooted in your discoveries. Consider how this approach propels you forward and moulds your strategy.

Reflect on how the entire process of calculating depth has influenced your approach to the task or goal at hand and consider any realisations or insights that have emerged because of this process. How have these newfound understandings shaped your actions and outcomes in your day-to-day endeavours? Think about how you can continue to utilise depth calculation techniques to tackle challenges and facilitate your growth and progress.

Engaging in reflection and writing can help you uncover the hidden corners of your subconscious mind effectively. Therefore, it is beneficial to utilise introspection for growth. Establish steps based on your reflections and monitor your progress consistently. Incorporating these strategies into your routine can aid you in achieving your goals and fostering changes.

A powerful tool for understanding your thoughts and making significant changes through careful consideration is at your disposal here. By delving into the depths of your thoughts and emotions and gaining an understanding of them, will enable you to craft targeted strategies and achievable steps to propel your goals and self-improvement efforts forward. Embrace this approach as an element in your journey towards success and transformation.

Summary & Practice

Exploring the concept of calculating depth at level and improving the Inquiry.

- Enhance your self-awareness by paying attention to your thoughts and emotions and take time to ponder the motivations behind them.

- Explore the workings of your thoughts by delving into areas of your life where you desire understanding or change.
- Consider pausing for a moment to reflect on viewpoints that may arise and acknowledge the influences that impact your decision-making process.
- Delve into your mind to uncover hidden fears and emotions that lie beneath the surface of your subconscious thoughts.
- Delve into challenges.
- Ask thought provoking questions to guide your exploration in uncovering the root causes behind them.
- Explore the recurring themes and patterns to understand the reasons behind your choices deeply.
- Transforming knowledge into steps.
- Break down your comprehension into a series of actions aimed at addressing the challenges you are facing.
- Make sure to develop a strategy that integrates these observations into your daily schedule and track your progress over time.

Consider the effects of employing these strategies on your decisions and outcomes. Continue refining your approach. By incorporating these habits into your routine and lifestyle will help you better comprehend the hidden patterns that shape your actions and choices on a subconscious level. This newfound awareness can give you the ability to make decisions that can lead to significant positive transformations in your life.

Chapter 7

Depth vs Breadth

The intention of Chapter 7 - Depth vs Breadth, is to inspire a change in how you make decisions by guiding you to strike an equilibrium between exploring different avenues and delving deeply into critical areas that offer the most potential impact. This chapter prompts you to move beyond ponderings and discover how to broaden your horizons while immersing yourself in the most effective tactics. By embracing both breadth and depth in your approach you empower yourself to maximise your resources and take actions that yield substantial and enduring outcomes. The aim is to help you harness the power of your thoughts effectively to discover deeper dimensions of personal development and change.

As a chess player facing a tough opponent in a high stakes game scenario that demands intense focus and strategic thinking must decide between delving deep into one line of play to analyse every move, or spreading attention across various lines to determine the best strategic advantage. Showcasing the delicate balance required to master your subconscious mind effectively.

In order to control your mind effectively it is important to grasp the equilibrium between breadth and exploring different options at depth. Delving deep into specific areas. Like in chess were concentrating on a single move without considering other possibilities can restrict your choices in life too. Understanding the balance of breadth versus depth, enables you to have a wider viewpoint while also concentrating intensely on specific aspects when needed.

Think about a challenge or goal you're facing right now and consider the various ways you could tackle it with different levels of commitment and focus on mind. Take a moment to picture yourself exploring each option briefly in your mind. What approach seems appealing to you now and which paths seem tougher or less significant to pursue? Trust your instincts as you make your decisions.

When you consider options thoroughly you are looking into all your choices extensively to see which one or two decisions need more attention and contemplation. Focusing deeply in areas helps you obtain profound understanding and develop plans suited to your objectives.

Have you ever thought about tapping into your subconscious by balancing between exploring different avenues and delving deeply into specific areas when necessary? Embracing the idea of breadth versus depth can enhance your ability to nurture and control your mind effectively – similar to how strategic thinking in chess involves analysing multiple moves to limit the opponents' options and devise a winning plan.

Imagine yourself in the shoes of a chess player mentioned earlier. Tasked with considering ways to address a personal challenge at hand. Picture yourself taking a moment to explore strategies for tackling this issue, each requiring varying levels of commitment and focus. Envision yourself examining each option before ultimately deciding which path to pursue with care and diligence.

Take a moment to jot down your thoughts on each option you have in front of you, considering which ones stand out as potentially beneficial and which ones appear more challenging or irrelevant to your goals. How does your gut feeling guide you in making decisions about these options?

Consider your perspective. How you weighed different options carefully. Why did certain decisions stand out from the rest for you? Understanding how you assess options and decide where to focus your energies can offer valuable insights into your subconscious thoughts and decision-making tendencies.

Start by identifying areas where you would like to see growth or progress in order to strike a good balance between the scope and depth of educating your subconscious mind. Examine techniques or approaches considering how they may impact and be relevant. Once you have explored your options thoroughly choose a few key areas to delve further into. Effectively managing your focus is crucial for optimising your endeavours and achieving the desired results.

Embracing both breadth and depth is crucial when it comes to understanding your mind fully. You should explore options and focus on the ones that seem most probable. This approach will enable you to devise a plan that optimises your resources and fosters personal growth. Adopting this mindset can assist you in navigating your subconscious and initiating profound enduring changes.

When delving into this idea further it is vital to know when to broaden your view and when to zoom in on specifics. Maintaining an equilibrium between exploring avenues and delving into the most favourable ones is key to personal growth. This equilibrium enables you to enhance your development by considering numerous possibilities and devoting time to aspects requiring more in-depth exploration.

Exploring avenues and approaches available to us in a given situation or problem-solving scenario allows us to understand what choices we have at our disposal fully. This process then empowers us to assess and determine which strategies hold the promise or likelihood of success. Nevertheless, once we have pinpointed the feasible pathways forward, it is essential that we delve deeper into these options, as this will enable us to tackle any underlying challenges or issues that may arise along the way.

To put this idea into action in your life, think about an aspect of your life that you would like to improve or change for the betterment of yourself and others around you. Brainstorm a variety of approaches that could help you achieve this goal. Assess each approach based on how effective it could be in bringing about positive changes and how closely it matches your desired outcomes. After weighing your options carefully and considering all aspects involved in each approach, choose one or two strategies that stand out to you as the most promising and delve deeper into understanding them further.

When you do this task effectively you are considering a range of options while also delving deep into the details to ensure that your attention is directed towards the tactics that hold promise for achieving significant results. Balancing between exploring options and focusing on specific topics is essential for personal growth and efficient resource management.

Exploring a variety of options allows for an understanding of available choices and helps in deciding where to focus efforts and identify intriguing opportunities. Conversely, diving into specific subjects aids in solving core issues and developing targeted solutions.

How can this concept be put into practice effectively? Begin by exploring approaches to addressing your challenges. Consider the impacts of each option and determine which aligns best with your goals. Once you have identified the promising paths forward, focus on these specific areas and employ thorough analysis to identify and address the underlying issues.

Take a moment to think about an area in your life that you'd like to improve or grow in. It could be anything from relationships to career goals or personal development. Jot down a range of solutions for this challenge and then assess each option for its potential impact on your life goals, and how feasible it is to implement those changes effectively.

After considering your options and selecting a couple that seems promising for your goals ahead, think about how you plan to apply these methods and determine the resources required. Establish a timeline to delve deeper into their exploration, keep tabs on your progress and adjust your approach based on your encounters and insights gained along the way.

Reflect on your process of evaluating and selecting strategies in the past. How did considering options help you discover the most intriguing paths? Did immersing yourself in techniques teach you valuable lessons? By focusing on efficient approaches, you can strike a balance between breadth and depth and effectively manage your endeavours to enhance your personal growth.

When you reach a level of expertise in a subject area understanding the balance between breadth and depth of knowledge is key to effectively managing your energy reserves smartly. It requires evaluating options and then honing in on the areas that promise the greatest opportunities for development. By following this approach you can make the most of your endeavours and experience profound and enduring change.

To start applying this idea in life, first figure out a personal goal or issue you're dealing with right now. It could be anything that's on your mind currently. Then jot down three ways or approaches you could take to tackle this goal head-on. For each method you come up with think about how effective it could be and whether it fits well with what you are aiming for in the picture. Once you've weighed all your options go ahead pick out the most promising ones and craft a detailed plan to dive deeper into these possibilities.

Consider how you plan to put these tactics into action and the tools or resources required to do so effectively. As you progress further along this path of action-taking and learning things along the way, it's important to keep tabs on your advancement and tweak your methods in response to fresh perspectives or observations.

Thinking about how balancing a range of ideas and focusing deeply has shaped your efforts toward reaching this objective is key here. How did looking into possibilities aid in pinpointing the most encouraging direction? What perspectives did you acquire from delving deeply into a couple of tactics? This method enables you to handle your tasks effectively making sure you utilise your time and energy wisely.

Utilise the idea of breadth versus depth by exploring various techniques and methods to enhance your understanding and possibilities in different areas of interest, like reflection practice or guided visualisation exercises. Select your points and delve deep into these methods to address core issues and achieve your goals effectively. Adapt your approach regularly based on your progress and newfound insights.

Mastering your mind is greatly influenced by finding a balance between breadth and depth of understanding within yourself. By exploring options and focusing primarily on the most favourable solutions you can enhance your efforts and achieve greater success. Embracing this idea can help you take charge of your growth, strengthen your ability to overcome challenges and move closer to accomplishing your goals.

Opting between breadth and depth involves making decisions about where to focus your efforts effectively. Pushing for change requires evaluating various options, resorting to the most probable ones and delving deeply into these specific areas.

Why is it important to apply your efforts and resources in handling challenges that impact your personal growth positively? By finding a balance between the breadth and depth of your approach you can enhance the effectiveness of your actions and achieve significant and enduring results.

How would you use this approach in practice? To start with, identify the areas in your life that you wish to improve or change. Then, explore methods or strategies for addressing these areas.

Explore fields and evaluate their relevance and potential impact. Pick a couple of methods to focus on in depth and establish a plan to implement these concepts effectively. Monitor your progress and adjust your approach based on feedback and personal experiences as needed.

What personal goal or task are you currently working toward? Outline three approaches you could use to tackle a goal or challenge effectively. Be sure to assess each option's impact feasibility and alignment with your primary objectives.

Develop a strategy for delving into the intriguing concepts further by considering how to apply these methods effectively and identifying the necessary tools for the task, while monitoring your progress regularly within your plan and adjusting your approach based on new insights and observations that arise along the way.

Reflect on the process of developing and executing your plan. How did your approach to achieving your goal evolve based on assessment and strategy selection? Upon scrutinising tactics, did you unearth any insights? Leveraging the concept of breadth versus depth, can empower you to manage your endeavours and yield meaningful and enduring outcomes.

To incorporate the idea of exploring versus going deep into specific areas of interest or study effectively, keep trying out various methods and approaches regularly for a well-rounded understanding and experience. Assess the options to you and decide upon the ones that capture your attention the most through self-reflective activities, like journaling or guided visualisation. Develop a strategy centred around these practices and monitor your progress to ensure you are moving towards your goals. Adapt your approach based on your experiences and newfound insights as you navigate through your journey.

Harnessing the power of your mind and fostering personal growth relies on embracing a wide-ranging rather than in-depth method of exploration and learning. To make progress it is crucial to explore various avenues and focus particularly on those that show the most potential. By adopting this approach you can enhance your ability to overcome challenges and achieve your goals effectively.

In this section we explored the concept of balancing breadth and depth when it comes to mastering your mind. By considering options and focusing on the most effective strategies you can enhance your efforts and achieve lasting success.

Reflect upon a goal or task that you are currently working towards as a final step in your process of self-improvement or achievement. Consider methods and focus primarily on those that show the most potential emphasising breadth over depth in your analysis. Develop a plan outlining the application of these strategies and monitor your progress closely. Reflect upon how this approach influences your ability to achieve your goal and facilitate personal growth.

Remember when you considered the balance between breadth and depth in your approach overall? Exploring methods and focusing specifically on certain areas provided you with what kind of understanding? How did incorporating this idea impact the way you went about achieving your goals? Consider how you can continue to utilise this strategy to support your growth and navigate future challenges effectively.

Engaging in reflection and journaling can assist in maintaining momentum and effectively applying the balance between broad exploration and in-depth focus by experimenting with various methods and perspectives, meticulously strategising around the most intriguing concepts monitoring progress over time, adapting strategies based on experiences and newfound insights.

In order to unlock the power of your subconscious and achieve growth, it is important to strike a balance between exploring various avenues and focusing on the ones that hold the most promise for lasting transformation. Embrace this concept as crucial in your journey towards achieving success and self-improvement.

Summary & Practice

Before settling on a strategy, it is advisable to explore options to see what works best in various situations. Exploring the balance between breadth and depth in understanding.

- Boost your progress by finding a harmony between exploring paths and diving deeply into essential areas.
- Consider utilising aids or engaging in self-reflective exercises to explore different possibilities and identify those worth exploring in more depth.
- Improve your game plan.
- Seek for ways to tackle challenges or goals.
- Assess the impact and practicality of each option based on your objectives.
- After carefully pondering all your options, look at the top choices to address core issues and achieve long-lasting results.

- Implement depth and scope through action.
- Focus on managing your tasks by exploring different possibilities and concentrating on areas that show the most potential for growth.
- Develop a strategy to explore these approaches thoroughly while keeping track of your progress and adjusting your techniques as needed.

Try to strike a balance between exploring subjects and diving deep into specific areas when organising tasks efficiently and achieving more significant results. By embracing both the idea of exploring opportunities and focusing deeply on promising strategies in your life journey, it allows for optimal personal growth and resource management leading to transformative outcomes that endure over time.

Chapter 8

Game Plan

The intention of Chapter 8 - Game Plan, is to empower you to gain control over your thoughts by preparing in advance and tackling the hurdles that hinder your progress towards achieving your objectives effectively. This chapter encourages you to view your mind as a tactical game where triumph doesn't solely rely on actions taken, but also on foreseeing and managing internal opponents like fears, doubts and self-defeating actions. By devising a strategy to tackle these obstacles directly you empower yourself to take control of yourself and remain concentrated on attaining enduring personal development and triumph.

Imagine yourself as a chess player facing a formidable adversary, on the board of life's game. As the match unfolds before you and strategies are put into play, you come to the realisation that triumph doesn't rely on your moves but also on your ability to foresee your opponent's next moves. Now envision employing this idea in order to become the master of your subconscious realm. Picture how comprehending and predicting the ambitions of your adversaries. Those internal uncertainties, fears, and hindrances could aid you in overcoming them with greater efficacy and success.

To take control of your mind it starts with acknowledging that internal hurdles are akin to invisible adversaries within your thoughts. Obstacles like procrastination or self-doubt that wield significant influence and may impede your journey towards achieving personal aspirations.

Take a moment to imagine a goal that's important to you, and that you are actively pursuing right now in your life journey. Think about the struggles and doubts that could potentially surface on this path. Maybe it's the fear of failing, battling with self-critical thoughts or putting off important tasks. Envision yourself acknowledging these obstacles even before they arise. How will you get ready to confront them head on? What approaches would you adopt to triumph over these challenges?

When you anticipate challenges ahead of time and develop tactics to keep yourself motivated and on track, you are laying the groundwork for understanding your inner thoughts better and handling obstacles more effectively when they come your way.

Anticipating an opponent's plans and intentions requires more than reacting to their actions alone. It involves recognising and addressing the hidden thoughts and emotions that may hinder your goals achievement in training the subconscious mind. Proactively addressing these conflicts allows you to steer your mental processes towards favourable outcomes and remove potential obstacles.

Take a moment to shut your eyes and take a breath in. Envision yourself tackling a significant personal goal head on with determination and focus in mind. Think about the challenges and doubts that may arise along the way. Whether its struggling with procrastination or battling self-doubt or feeling anxious about the possibility of failure.

Picture yourself anticipating these challenges in advance preparing for them proactively and effectively addressing them when they arise with others as adversaries or competitors in mind. Imagine yourself implementing these strategies and overcoming the obstacles successfully.

Take a moment to study this aid carefully and reflect on the insights that guided you in understanding how to anticipate and manage internal struggles effectively.

Remember when you visualised and considered how to approach challenges internally what made you choose the strategies you envisioned in the first place? Understanding how to anticipate and manage your struggles can provide valuable insight into controlling your subconscious mind.

As you work on understanding and preparing for challenges that arise from within yourself, it is crucial to notice the recurring ways in which these hurdles present themselves. Like a proficient chess player who studies their rivals' strategies you should observe your own patterns of thinking to grasp how doubts or fears show up internally. This mindfulness helps you proactively tackle obstacles and develop plans to tackle them early on before they become major roadblocks.

Why is this so crucial? Being able to foresee hurdles helps you come up with proactive solutions ahead of time before these issues become problematic. By identifying the indicators of self-sabotage procrastination or negative thoughts you can promptly address them to avoid any disruptions to your advancement. This looking strategy helps you stay on track with your objectives and sustains your drive.

When putting this idea into action in your life consider a goal that matters to you and recall moments when inner struggles such as fear of failure or uncertainty held you back in the past. Devise a strategy to tackle these obstacles proactively before they become major roadblocks. For instance, if procrastination is a recurring challenge for you, establish deadlines and provide yourself with incentives for meeting them. Alternatively, if self-doubt is a hurdle, engage in affirmations to strengthen your confidence in your capabilities.

When you plan ahead with these strategies in place, it makes it easier to handle any obstacles that come up later on. In this way you can stay on track and keep yourself motivated throughout the process.

Identify challenges that may arise while pursuing your goals and prepare in advance to address them effectively. Such as procrastination or self-doubt. By implementing strategies ahead of time to mitigate these obstacles and stay on track towards success. For instance, if you foresee procrastination as an issue set up a structured timeline with incentives and deadlines to help maintain focus and motivation. Regularly adapt your methods based on your past experiences for ongoing improvement.

To truly master your subconscious you need to anticipate and address any conflicts that may arise along the way preparing yourself for potential challenges is key in navigating your thoughts effectively and achieving your goals with greater success. Take on this approach to enhance your ability to overcome turmoil and stay focused on what you aim to achieve.

Anticipating your opponent's strategies involves understanding their moves and preparing for them in advance within the realm of training the subconscious mind, by recognising and addressing any internal factors that may hinder your progress.

Being prepared for problems enables you to plan and implement strategies before these obstacles fully manifest themselves, which in turn keeps you focused on your goals and helps maintain your momentum going forward in a productive manner. Understanding the underlying motivations of those within your organisation can assist you in staying focused and effectively mitigating any risks that may arise.

How could someone put this idea into practice? Begin by identifying internal barriers that may arise when pursuing personal goals. Reflect on past experiences to identify patterns or recurring difficulties. Develop proactive strategies to address these issues before they escalate. If procrastination is a recurring issue for you, take the time to create a detailed action plan and set regular checkpoints to hold yourself accountable.

Consider a goal you are currently working towards and identify any potential internal challenges you may encounter such as lack of motivation or confidence and fear of failing to accomplish it. Develop a strategy for each obstacle to address them proactively before they escalate into hurdles in your path to success.

Carefully plan out how you will incorporate these strategies into your routine, include goals like setting up a rewards system to stay motivated and using positive affirmations to combat self-doubt. Consider how employing these methods can help you anticipate and manage struggles more effectively.

Reflect on how you identified and resolved conflicts in the past and consider how your approach evolved as you developed strategies over time. What insights have you gained about managing challenges? Being prepared for obstacles can enhance your ability to stay on track and achieve your objectives.

Make sure to review your progress and adjust your plans as needed to anticipate and address any internal issues effectively. If you find that certain challenges are persisting longer than expected, consider modifying your approach or seeking assistance like guidance or support. Maintain a positive enquiring mindset and use your insights to continuously improve your strategies for overcoming personal obstacles.

Mastering your subconscious largely relies on anticipating hurdles and being prepared for them in advance enabling you to stay committed to your goals and maintain momentum effortlessly.

This proactive approach enhances your ability to navigate challenges effectively leading to lasting personal growth and transformation.

To fully unlock the potential of your mind at an advanced level entails more than just foreseeing internal obstacles. It also involves crafting a detailed strategy to confront them head on by recognising patterns of scepticism or uncertainty and devising specific tactics to conquer them effectively with the aim of turning your inner struggles into avenues for personal development.

When implementing this idea in a life scenario. Select a personal goal you are currently working towards. List any challenges you face or may face in the future like lack of drive or self-doubt. For each hurdle you expect to meet head on come up with a concrete strategy. For instance, if fear of failing trips you often, you could jot down affirmations daily to boost your confidence and strength. If delaying tasks is a problem for you set realistic deadlines for each task on your list.

Let's start by laying out a schedule for putting these plans into action. This way as you go along the process be sure to check in on how things are going and tweak your methods based on what you learn from your journey. Reflect on how being prepared for and dealing with these challenges inside has impacted your focus and advancement towards achieving your objective.

When you tackle issues head on from within yourself proactively you can have influence over how your mind works and reach enduring success in the long run. Take a moment to think about how this method has influenced your advancement. Did thinking ahead about obstacles keep you focused on your path to success? How did your method of reaching your target shift because of this forward-thinking approach?

Incorporating the concept of anticipation involves understanding the motives behind your internal challenges and creating strategies to effectively manage them proactively. This approach allows you to have more influence over your thought processes and achieve your goals successfully.

Why is anticipating strategically important in business and life alike? It enables you to address obstacles before they become major hurdles, thereby minimising their impact on your progress. Gaining a deep understanding of your inner challenges and taking proactive steps can assist you in maintaining focus and staying aligned with your objectives.

One way to utilise foresight is by reflecting on previous occurrences and identifying patterns in your personal dilemmas, before devising solutions that incorporate proactive approaches to address them effectively. Also, it's important to re-assess and modify your strategies based on your progress and learning experiences.

Select an objective you're striving for and specify any inner challenges you've faced or anticipate encountering along the way to achieving it. Develop a strategy that outlines approaches for addressing each obstacle effectively. For example, if you struggle with self-confidence draft a list of empowering statements. Establish daily routines incorporating them into your routine.

Execute your plan of action. Assess your progress over the course of several months' timeframe. Reflect upon how your methods are helping you to stay focused towards your goals and manage any inner challenges that arise. Adapt your approach based off of what you learn and encounter along the way.

Reflect on how your methods for managing conflicts fared in practice and evolved to adapt to anticipated challenges en route to your goals. What adjustments did you make to your approach based on encounters with obstacles? By recognising and confronting internal hurdles, you can enhance your ability to achieve objectives and navigate challenging circumstances effectively.

Make sure to review and enhance your strategies to maintain progress and effectively address any internal hurdles you encounter along the way. Seek advice and support from individuals such as mentors or coaches for fresh ideas and guidance. Take an approach to tackling internal obstacles by adapting your plans according to your experiences and growth journey.

Mastering your thoughts and personal growth relies on being prepared for potential challenges ahead of time. Strategically foreseeing internal issues can reduce their impact and maintain focus on your goals. This proactive approach can enhance your ability to overcome obstacles and achieve lasting success.

This section explored the concept of anticipating hurdles and strategies for effectively managing them, in order to maintain momentum and focus on your goals.

Reflect upon a goal or challenge you are addressing as a final workout session, employing the proactive approach by identifying potential internal obstacles and devising strategies to move past them confidently and effectively. Utilise your devised strategies, track your progress over a period of time and reflect upon how this proactive approach has aided you in conquering internal hurdles and achieving your desired objective.

Reflect on the process of preparing for and handling challenges as a whole. What insights did you gain about your ability to stay committed to your goals and surmount obstacles? How do you plan to integrate these insights into your approach to achieving objectives? Consider how you can continue to embrace this concept to aid in your personal growth and navigate hurdles with greater finesse.

Make sure to review your plans to maintain progress and effectively address any internal obstacles that may arise. Don't hesitate to seek additional assistance when needed! Approach challenges with a positive enquiring mindset and use your insights to continuously improve how you tackle them. Stay focused on your goals. Adjust your plans as you progress and gain experience.

One effective approach to managing your thoughts and achieving personal growth is to anticipate and address internal conflicts that may arise within you. Preparing for obstacles can reduce their impact and allow you to focus on your goals more effectively. Embrace this strategy to enhance your ability to navigate internal resistance and achieve lasting success.

Summary & Practice

Within the battlefield of your thoughts, dwell opponents such as procrastination and self-doubt that impede your journey towards achievement and fulfilment. Prepare for challenges that might arise from within and plan on how to address them proactively.

- Develop strategies to stay focused and motivated by anticipating challenges in advance.
- Improve your forecasting skills and strategic analysis.
- Contemplate past encounters to identify trends in the way personal struggles manifest themselves internally.
- Find ways to address these obstacles before they impede your progress.
- Try using affirmations daily and establish clear deadlines to tackle common challenges, like procrastination and self-doubt, in your professional or personal endeavours.
- Develop a plan for attaining expertise.
- Could you share the difficulties you've encountered or anticipate encountering along with your strategies for overcoming each one in detail?

- Craft a timetable for implementing these strategies and regularly evaluate your progress.
- Consider how facing hurdles impacted your focus and achievements in attaining your goals.

By embracing this forward-thinking mindset in your life, it helps you to take charge of your thoughts and emotions effectively so that obstacles within you no longer hinder your progress and development endeavours. This proactive stance empowers you to turn your struggles into chances for personal advancement and achievement.

Chapter 9

Play

The intention of Chapter 9 - Play, is to change how you view life, by adopting an attitude as a different approach to living life fully and freely after learning techniques to mould your subconscious and conquer the challenges in the previous sections. Play, suggests taking the leap into a realm of endless opportunities where you dictate the rules of your own journey, encourages leaving behind past limitations unlocking creativity and embracing life with curiosity and joy. The aim is to inspire you to see your path as a journey where you play the roles of both creator and protagonist in shaping a tomorrow brimming with boundless opportunities.

Great job! You've finished a journey of growth and now finding yourself successfully completed, the final part of your adventure today is not just an end but a beginning of an exciting new chapter where you take charge as the main character in your story. Welcome to Chapter 9 called "Play," where the possibilities are truly limitless and you get to create your own game rules.

At this stage you have honed your strategic skills and delved deep into understanding your inner workings with expertise. You've gained self-awareness by examining your behaviours and beliefs. Learned to appreciate the wisdom offered by your gut feelings.

These valuable skills have primed you for the stage where you can put what you've learned into action to craft a promising future for yourself.

Imagine the thrill of crafting your life carefully organising every element with the precision of a skilled chess player planning their next move. What dreams have you longed to pursue? What new interests are you eager to explore? Now is your opportunity to unleash your creativity and see the world through a lens of potential.

Welcome to this new chapter in your life! Remember to enjoy yourself and approach each challenge with a sense of exploration and wonderment. Let your creativity run free without being held by the past constraints. Embrace the possibilities of a future shaped by your decisions and take charge of your destiny.

Life is like a game without rules. It's all up to you to shape your path as the architect of your journey and the brave explorer of new horizons where unexpected transformations await.

Player! It's time for you to make your mark on the world as the stage is set for you now. Approach this chapter with an open heart and a positive outlook while firmly believing in your ability to achieve your dreams and goals. Are you ready, for this journey that is about to unfold before you?

In life's journey and in the game of chess one must appreciate the importance of controlling one's thoughts to advance towards their aspirations successfully. The process commences with comprehending the workings of your mind—a potent yet often unnoticed influencer that shapes your thinking patterns, choices, and actions. Previous sections delved into methods, approaches, and perspectives on leveraging the potential of your subconscious to foster impactful and enduring transformations in your life. In this section of this book we will review the main ideas discussed in each chapter and offer you practical guidance on how to implement these strategies in your own endeavours.

The cornerstone of any exploration is being mindful. Being conscious of the patterns that drive your actions and the deep-seated beliefs that influence how you respond to life's trials and tribulations. As detailed in Chapter 1 called "The Opponent" your subconscious often serves as an opponent by erecting barriers to achievement through self-doubt anxieties and automatic negative thoughts. The initial step in mastering your subconscious is acknowledging these hurdles and realising that they are not set in stone but rather outdated narratives that you hold the power to alter. Establishing an understanding of these underlying patterns lays the groundwork for all events.

Building upon this understanding laid out in Chapter 2 titled "Contemplation", various techniques were introduced to further explore and grasp these patterns using tools like keeping a journal and practicing mindfulness and visualisation exercises regularly. By reflecting on your experiences on a consistent basis through these methods mentioned earlier in the chapter. You start noticing the interplay between your thought's feelings and actions more clearly. The act of contemplation enables you to observe repetitive responses and pinpoint the fundamental beliefs that underlie them. When you practice mindfulness regularly and focus on being present in the moment, it helps you to pause and think before reacting to situations in a more purposeful manner rather than just reacting impulsively.

In the chapter titled "Resources" you'll find a range of methods like Cognitive Behavioural Therapy (CBT), Neuro Linguistic Programming (NLP), and Emotional Freedom Techniques (EFT), that provide effective ways to reshape your subconscious mind by challenging negative thoughts and changing limiting beliefs and ingrained patterns actively. The aim is not to comprehend how your subconscious works but to take action by utilising these tools to develop new positive mental frameworks that align with your aspirations.

In the chapter titled "Intuition" we probed into the idea of intuitive judgment and how honing this ability can improve your capacity to tackle life's obstacles effectively. It is about accessing your wisdom that accompanies logical thinking. To strike a balance in dealing with scenarios it is essential to rely on both your instincts and analytical reasoning. By refining your discernment skills you develop a stronger bond with your inner self and discover how to rely on it as a compass in making choices.

Recognising and understanding the patterns in your thoughts and actions plays a role in our lives as highlighted in Chapter 5 titled "Patterns & Strategies". Like how a chess player studies their opponents moves to forecast future results, identifying patterns in your own life can help you anticipate challenges and possibilities ahead of time. Keeping a journal and regularly reflecting on your experiences can help you uncover these patterns and gain insights into how your past decisions shape your choices. By delving into these patterns and analysing them thoroughly, you can develop strategies to adjust your behaviour in ways that align with your objectives.

Delving into the depths of your thoughts and behaviours is what the concept of depth calculation in Chapter 6 focuses on – it involves unearthing the underlying reasons hidden within your subconscious mind that drive your actions and beliefs forward with intent and purpose. In this chapter's exploration of depth calculation emphasises the significance of looking beyond surface motivations to uncover the values and emotions that guide your choices and decisions in life. Through the practice of depth calculation methodically peeling back layer by layer to expose the core truths about yourself – you develop an awareness of the intricate interplay between internal motives and external actions leading to more deliberate and well-informed decision-making processes.

In Chapter 7 titled "Depth vs Breadth" we look into the concept of finding a harmony between delving into one topic and exploring various alternatives. Similar to how a chess player must decide whether to focus on a tactic or think about broader options available to them in the game's strategy. You also need to find a balance between diving deep into a single aspect and considering a wider range in your personal progress. While immersing yourself fully in tackling an obstacle can bring profound insights, broadening your viewpoint by looking at different methods can spark new perspectives and solutions. To enhance your development and improve decision-making skills effectively, ensure a good balance of depth and breadth in your approach.

In Chapter 8 "Game Plan", the focus was on the significance of foreseeing hurdles and creating effective strategies to tackle them head on, just like a chess player strategizes against their adversaries' moves. Mastering control over your subconscious involves being able to predict and address potential obstacles, like procrastination or self-doubt before they become roadblocks in your path to success. By preparing for these challenges in advance and devising a plan that considers potential setbacks ahead of time, allows you to maintain your concentration and drive towards achieving your objectives. Having a game plan that is designed to anticipate setbacks enables you to stay proactive in overcoming resistance and keep moving forward even when faced with difficulties.

As you have gone through these chapters and learned a lot of techniques and tips to control your mind effectively over time. With continual practice in your daily life, like a chess player refining their skills with each game played aiming to enhance your ability to manage and reshape your subconscious thoughts and behaviours steadily as you invest time and energy into it. Initiate the process by building mindfulness – pay attention to your thoughts and feelings without any bias or criticism. Incorporate techniques such as keeping a journal and practicing mindfulness and visualisation to gain deeper insight into your internal patterns.

After gaining an understanding of your subconscious thoughts and feelings take action by engaging proactively in addressing them. Use healing methods such as Cognitive Behavioural Therapy (CBT) or Emotional Freedom Techniques (EFT) to question negative beliefs and transform restrictive patterns. Rely on your instincts when making choices and aim for a balance between deep exploration and broad growth. Reflect regularly on your journey noting trends in achievements and obstacles. Utilise in depth analysis to uncover the underlying reasons for your difficulties and create effective strategies to tackle any internal barriers that may arise.

Understanding and controlling your mind is a journey that never really ends—it demands patience and self-kindness as well as the courage to face challenging realities head-on. Embrace the wisdom and strategies you gather along the way to experience personal development growth and achieve greater strength and success. Stay dedicated to honing your approach and celebrate each accomplishment as progress towards harnessing the potent energies residing within you. Approach this adventure with a sense of wonder and persistence. You will discover that your inner mind can be a partner in reaching your aspirations.

Bonus!

Prescript for Releasing Negative Programming and Scarcity Mindset

Begin by finding a quiet space where you can relax completely, free from distractions. Sit or lie down comfortably and take a few deep breaths. As you inhale, draw in peace and relaxation, as you exhale release any tensions or stress. Allow your body to become still and your mind to become open and receptive. Read through the following visualisation and allow the images and thoughts to reach your own experience if you identify, if not visualise the areas similar to your story.

Visualize: Picture a timeline of your life stretching out before you. See moments from your past where feelings of lack, scarcity, or fear around money might have taken root. Acknowledge and accept. I acknowledge that I am a product of my past, but I am not bound by it. I recognise that some beliefs, formed during my early years, were based on experiences of scarcity and limitation. These beliefs served a purpose at one time, but they no longer serve me now. Imagine these limiting beliefs as dark clouds or chains that have been holding you back. See yourself gently but firmly removing these chains or blowing the clouds away with a breath of release. See new, empowering beliefs taking the place of the old ones. Picture these as bright, golden light filling the spaces where the dark clouds or chains once were. As I release these outdated beliefs, I replace them with empowering thoughts that reflect my true worth and potential. Imagine meeting your younger self. Embrace them with love and kindness, reassuring them that the hardships they faced are over. Tell them that it is safe to let go of fear and to embrace abundance. As these moments appear, acknowledge them without judgment. Understand that these experiences were simply a reflection of your circumstances at that time, not of your true potential. I send love and healing to my younger self, the part of me that may have absorbed these limiting beliefs. I assure my inner child that we are safe, that abundance is our birthright, and that we are fully supported in this life. See yourself as the person you wish to become—prosperous, confident, and at peace with money. Imagine yourself moving through life with ease, attracting wealth naturally. This process is complete. The old, limiting beliefs have been fully released, and my new, empowering beliefs are firmly rooted in my subconscious mind. I am free from past limitations and fully open to the abundant future that awaits me. Imagine a seal of golden light surrounding you, locking in these new beliefs and protecting you from any negativity or doubt. Return to awareness. Take a deep breath, and as you exhale, slowly bring your awareness back to the present moment. Wiggle your fingers and toes and gently stretch, when you are ready. Feel the lightness and confidence that comes from knowing you have cleared away the old and made space for the new.

Affirmations:

- I release all fear, doubt, and scarcity from my mind and body.
- I let go of any belief that money is hard to come by or that I am not deserving of wealth.
- I now choose to release all limiting beliefs about money and abundance that were programmed into my subconscious during my childhood or any other time in my life.
- These beliefs no longer define me.
- I let them go with love and gratitude, knowing they are no longer needed.
- I am capable, deserving, and worthy of unlimited abundance.
- I am open to receiving wealth in all forms, and I trust the universe to provide for me generously.

- I am worthy of wealth.
- I am deserving of success.
- I am open to the infinite possibilities that surround me.
- I nurture my inner child with love and compassion.
- Together, we move forward with confidence and joy, embracing the wealth that is ours to claim.
- I now step into my true identity as a creator of wealth and abundance.
- My mind is free from the chains of scarcity.
- My thoughts, actions, and beliefs are aligned with prosperity.
- I am empowered, confident, and in control of my financial destiny.
- I am a magnet for wealth.
- I am aligned with the energy of abundance.
- I create, attract, and enjoy wealth effortlessly.
- I am protected, guided, and abundantly blessed.
- My mind, body, and spirit are aligned with the wealth I deserve.

Daily Practice:

Morning Affirmation: Begin each day by revisiting this prescript. Reinforce your intention to live free from past limitations.

Evening Reflection: End your day by reflecting on any moments where old beliefs may have surfaced, and reaffirm your commitment to your new, empowering mindset.

By consistently practising this script, you will systematically clear away any residual negativity or scarcity programming, paving the way for sustained wealth creation and a mindset fully aligned with abundance.

The Beginning!

www.ingramcontent.com/pod-product-compliance
Lightning Source LLC
LaVergne TN
LVHW050600160826
845677LV00011B/2390

* 9 7 9 8 2 2 7 1 7 0 5 6 9 *